∞ *Tracing* ∞
Your Scottish Ancestors

General Register House

TRACING YOUR SCOTTISH
⌒ ANCESTORS ⌒

A GUIDE TO ANCESTRY RESEARCH IN THE
NATIONAL ARCHIVES OF SCOTLAND

The NATIONAL
ARCHIVES
of **SCOTLAND**

mercatpress
www.mercatpress.com

ISBN 1 841830 593

This third edition first published 2003 by
The National Archives of Scotland and
Mercat Press, 10 Coates Crescent, Edinburgh EH3 7AL
www.mercatpress.com

First published 1990, revised edition published 1997

British Library Cataloguing in Publication Data

A catalogue record for this is available from the British Library

Set in New Baskerville Bold and Bembo at Mercat Press

Printed and bound in Great Britain by
Bell & Bain Ltd., Glasgow

❧ *Contents* ❧

∾ *Illustrations* ∾

∽ *Preface* ∽

There are many books on Scottish family history. What makes this one unique is that it is written from the inside, with the knowledge and expertise of the people who look after the records. It distils the combined experience of generations of archivists, and will be equally of use to guide the novice and the expert family historian.

This is the third edition of this book, which has become one of the bestsellers of the National Archives of Scotland. In the 13-odd years since it first appeared, the world has changed considerably, but interest in family history has continued to grow steadily. Among the customers using our historical search rooms, two-thirds are now researching family history.

One of the things which has changed in the last few years is the increase in the use of computers and the Internet. These will not do family history for you, but they do make it easier. Nothing can beat the sheer excitement of using original records, of seeing the traces of our ancestors and learning to 'listen' to what they have to say. But for those who cannot easily come to Edinburgh to use the great treasures of the National Archives of Scotland and the General Register Office for Scotland, remote searching of documents by Internet is now possible. The two institutions, and the Court of the Lord Lyon, are working closely together to develop a single service for the Scottish family historian, available both in Edinburgh and remotely on the Internet.

I would like to thank John Randall, Registrar General, for permission to include the chapter dealing with records held by the General Register Office for Scotland.

Whether you come to search personally in the records, or work remotely from your home, this book will be an indispensable guide.

GEORGE P MACKENZIE
Keeper of the Records of Scotland

𝕔𝕠 *1* 𝕔𝕠

Introduction

They trace his steps till they can tell
His pedigree as weel's himsell
Robert Fergusson

1.1 You want to find your Scottish ancestors. This book is written specifically to help you to trace those ancestors who are mentioned in the documents preserved in the National Archives of Scotland, a primary location of records for family research.

Family group 1910, private collection.

The National Archives of Scotland

1.2   The National Archives of Scotland is the government department responsible for the custody and preservation of the records of the government of Scotland. It also has taken responsibility for and custody of the records of many non-government concerns, including church records and the records of some private families and businesses. Most of these records may be consulted by members of the public.

1.3   The National Archives of Scotland occupies two buildings in the centre of Edinburgh, close to the railway and bus stations. One building is General Register House, at the east end of Princes Street, opposite the Balmoral Hotel and the former General Post Office. A statue of the Duke of Wellington ('the man on the horse') guards the entrance to this building, which houses, as well as many records, two search rooms: the Legal Search Room and the Historical Search Room. As searching for your ancestors is regarded as historical research, you will use the Historical Search Room. If you want to see any of the records for a legal purpose, then you will use the Legal Search Room and be charged a fee. You will not be charged for doing historical research, but you must do your own research. The staff will advise you and try to answer all reasonable questions, but the rest is up to you. Hence this book!

1.4   The second building, West Register House, is situated in Charlotte Square, about a mile away from General Register House. It also contains a search room, the West Search Room, in which you may do historical research. The same rules, regulations and procedures apply to both Historical and West Search Rooms. Both are open from Monday to Friday, 09.00 – 16.45 hours, apart from certain public holidays and a period of annual stocktaking in November. At the time of writing an experiment is in place to offer late-evening opening at General Register House on Thursdays: please check the NAS website (*www.nas.gov.uk*) for details.

1.5   Confusingly, there is another building called New Register House, which is adjacent to General Register House but is not part of the National Archives of Scotland. This building houses the General Register Office for Scotland and the official records of births, marriages, deaths and census records. Although not directly within the bounds of this book, the records held there are of paramount importance to the family historian and are described in Chapter 4.

About this book

1.6   The first five chapters are introductory ones, which you should read before planning a visit to or writing to the National Archives of Scotland. The remaining chapters describe records in the National Archives of Scotland that might be of use to you in your search for your ancestors. In a sense, all records which name individuals may provide genealogical information, but we have tried to select and describe those which will be most useful. Chapters 7-11 concern records which should be of interest to all ancestor hunters: records of baptism, marriage, death, inheritance, landowning and tenancy. The remaining chapters describe records which concern particular activities or professions or situations; records which are less likely to specify relationships, though they may, but will add foliage to your family tree.

1.7   An attempt has been made to lead the reader step-by-step into the records, particularly those records described in the earlier chapters which should prove the most profitable. The intention is to enable you to do your research with decreasing reliance on the advice of the staff. Descriptions of procedures in the later pages of the book will assume that you have become familiar with the techniques of searching records.

1.8   As this book is intended specifically to help genealogical researchers, it does not cover all the records in the National Archives of Scotland or deal with all aspects of those records described. Legal concepts may be simplified in their description.

1.9   Do bear in mind that you will be using records which were drawn up for particular administrative or legal purposes. You will be using them for a different purpose (genealogy) so do not be disappointed if the information you are seeking is not available in the form in which you would like to find it. Perhaps we should warn you that any sort of historical research can be addictive and after a little practice you will find yourself becoming familiar with words and concepts from the world of your ancestors.

1.10   While reading this book, you may encounter unusual words. There will also be unfamiliar words in the records which you are going to search. It is useful get into the habit of using a dictionary, such as *The Concise Scots Dictionary* (Polygon at Edinburgh, 1999). You will also find in the records expressions which seem to us now to be pejorative, such as 'bastard' or 'lunatic'. Please try not to be offended by such phrases. However much we may dislike this today, these were the terms in use at the time and there is no point, for example, in referring readers to a 'register of psychiatric patients' when the record is called 'Register of Lunatics'.

1.11 Most of the published works we mention in this book should be available in the United Kingdom through a local library, perhaps by inter-library loan. The names of publishers are placed in brackets after the titles of recently-published books, but not out-of-print ones.

1.12 In our use of personal pronouns, we have described your ancestors as if they were all male. This is a matter of convenience and we apologise to those who are rightly offended. However, it is a sad fact that men are more likely to be named in the records than women.

1.13 Throughout the rest of this book, the National Archives of Scotland will be represented by the initials NAS. All paragraphs in the book are numbered and a reference to a paragraph from elsewhere in the book will be by its number. A reference to this paragraph would be simply 1.13.

Enquiries from a distance

1.14 While this book is primarily designed to help people to do their own research in the NAS, we hope that it will also help and guide those who are unable to come to Edinburgh, but who wish to trace their Scottish ancestry. While enquiries are welcome, the staff of the NAS, because of pressure of work, cannot carry out research on behalf of enquirers. Staff will provide advice and will answer specific enquiries. If you are unable to carry out your research yourself, you may wish to consider employing a professional searcher. NAS staff will send a list of those currently working in Scotland on request.

1.15 Please do not send any payment unless and until you are requested to do so.

1.16 All correspondence should be addressed to

The Keeper of the Records of Scotland
The National Archives of Scotland
H M General Register House
2 Princes Street
Edinburgh EHI 3YY
Scotland

The telephone number is 0131–535 1314 and the fax number is 0131–535 1360. The website address is *www.nas.gov.uk*.

E-mail enquiries should be sent to *enquiries@nas.gov.uk*.

❦ 2 ❦

First Steps in Family Research

2.1   The NAS will not be your first port of call when you decide to find out who your ancestors were. First ask your Aunt Jessie. In other words, begin with your own living family. There is usually at least one elderly relative who is interested in the family and acts as the family memory, though that memory may be reliable for only a couple of generations back. (Be wary of romantic family traditions that claim descent from the disinherited child of a nobleman or from the owner of a castle.) Some of your relatives may have preserved old family letters and documents such as birth certificates and wills. Also, if the family has lived in the same locality for some generations, it will be worth looking at gravestones in the local kirkyard or graveyard.

2.2   From this information, you will have a basis on which to build. If you live in Scotland, a visit to your local library is recommended. Even if you live in another country, your library may be able to obtain useful books for you. If your ancestors stayed for a long time in one area, familiarise yourself with that area, by means of studying local maps, e.g. Victorian large-scale Ordnance Survey maps; reading parish histories; checking if the local library has any street directories.

2.3   If your ancestor was genuinely a product of a noble or landed family, you should look at *The Scots Peerage* or *Burke's Peerage, Baronetage and Knightage* or *Burke's Landed Gentry*. Useful guides to printed sources on particular families are *Scottish Family History* by Margaret Stuart and Balfour Paul and *Scottish Family Histories* by J P S Ferguson (National Library of Scotland). Miss Ferguson has also produced a *Directory of Scottish Newspapers* (National Library of Scotland), which will tell you which Scottish libraries hold copies of a particular local newspaper. Similar information may be found in *NEWSPLAN: Report of the NEWSPLAN italics project in Scotland* (British Library). If an ancestor was a local dignitary, there may be an obituary of him in a local newspaper. The annual volumes of

Wedding photograph, 1930. (Private Collection)

the *Edinburgh Almanack* name office holders throughout Scotland since the mid-eighteenth century.

2.4 To find out information about an ancestor, you must know in what part of Scotland he lived. You must also have some knowledge of the administrative areas into which Scotland was divided. For centuries, the basic units were the parish, burgh, county and sheriffdom, and you should try to find out in which of these your ancestors may have lived. The General Register Office has produced a useful *Index of Scottish Place Names* (various editions), which lists the then inhabited places in Scotland, showing the county and parish in which each was located. If this publication is not available or you cannot find a place-name in it, try a pre-1975 gazetteer or a nineteenth-century edition of the *County Directory of Scotland,* which gives the nearest town and sometimes the county of inhabited places. A useful index of parishes, showing the related counties, sheriffdoms, commissary courts (see Chapter 8) and burghs is obtainable from the compiler Mrs A R Bigwood, Flat B, The Lodge, 2 East Road, North Berwick, EH39 4HN. Another alphabetical list of parishes, showing the sheriffdom, diocese, presbytery and commissariot of each is printed in *An Historical Catalogue of the Scottish Bishops* by Robert Keith (Edinburgh, 1824) and in *In Search of Scottish Ancestry* by Gerald Hamilton-Edwards (Phillimore). As the boundaries of parishes and other administrative areas did not remain the same throughout the centuries and human beings are often mobile, you should note the names of adjacent parishes and other areas in case you need to extend your search to them. There was a particularly significant alteration of county and parish boundaries in 1891.

2.5 If you want to find out about the history of your surname (as opposed to that of your family), look at *The Surnames of Scotland* by George F Black (New York Public Library). However, names can be a snare sometimes, as it is only in comparatively recent times that we have spelled names consistently.

2.6 An ancestor may have had the same surname as you, but spelled it differently. Clerks writing this surname down in official documents might spell it in yet other ways. Even with forenames, you have to be canny: e.g. Patrick and Peter used to be interchangeable names. But with forenames, you have a marvellous advantage in the Scottish practice of naming almost every child after a relative. Thus, it is reasonable to expect that an eldest son is named after his father's father, the second after his mother's father, the third after his own father, an eldest daughter after her mother's mother, the second after her father's mother, and the third after her own mother, and younger children after available uncles and aunts. A practice less convenient for us, however, was the naming of infants after elder brothers and sisters who had died: another snare for the genealogist.

2.7 Your preliminary investigation complete, you will probably now want to consider the resources available to the genealogist on the internet. See the next chapter for guidance. If you do not have access to the internet, it is perfectly possible to carry out research in the traditional manner. If you are in this position, you may wish to skip the next chapter and move to Chapter 4.

∽ 3 ∽

Tracing Scottish Ancestors on the Internet

3.1   We should start this chapter with a warning. The Internet has created ex-
pectations that with its help information can be found almost instantly, but
this is not always the case. By using the web, the fortunate family historian
can find descriptive catalogues that lead to images or transcripts of original
documents. While this is not true of every record group, work is constantly
advancing, in Scotland as elsewhere, to make copies available in this way to
assist historical research. But that is only part of the Internet's value.

3.2   As this book describes, there are many papers, registers, and volumes, files
and photos – together simply described as 'records' – of great potential to
Scottish genealogists. Such is the accumulation of records preserved from
generations past that catalogues of great numbers of collections have yet
to appear online. This is despite the mass of relevant material already
available in that way. Also, the genealogist is one of many users, although
an important one, to be considered when resources are being allocated to
increasing access to records online. Then there are practical and legal rea-
sons that prevent many records from being displayed on the web. It is
sadly the case that, sometimes, gaps exist in collections. In such circumstances the Internet again comes into its own. It helps to track down
alternative sources from which we may glean information. It acts as a tool
for individual family historians to plan what it is realistic for them to do in
exploring the resources of the archives, libraries and record centres of the
world and in our case Scotland. The downside is that the freedom of the
Internet itself creates a form of chaos, for example in the inevitable dupli-
cation of information that one finds on different gateways providing hun-
dreds of links to other sites.

3.3   In some circumstances the suggested outcome of your search for genealogical information on the Internet would be a visit to Scotland. For advice on

conducting a search from a distance see the NAS website at *www.nas.gov.uk*. If a visit is impractical, one option is to use a professional record searcher to do the work for you. Contact details for some searchers are found on, for example, Cyndi's List of Genealogy Sites on the Internet – *www.cyndislist.com/ scotland.htm#Professional*. Members of family history societies in areas of interest to you may help you in exchange for any assistance you can provide for them in return. You may also find that societies can for a moderate fee offer you the services of volunteers to help.

3.4   A reference to a website in this publication is not in itself an endorsement. Please note that some websites mentioned below make charges for the services they offer. In this short chapter we aim to give a flavour of what can be found and can do no more than mention a selection of sites. We have selected those created or supported by government bodies and Scottish archives and libraries; gateways giving family history links by category; and a further selection of sites to demonstrate a variety of record types and services on offer. Given the developments taking place here at the NAS, we are only too aware that information on particular websites and webpages can change, as can web addresses, and that sites come and go. Keep an eye on our website, *www.nas.gov.uk*, for developments in our own family history service.

The Scottish Archive Network

3.5   The Scottish Archive Network (SCAN) is a major co-operative venture of relevance to the family historian. SCAN is supported by the Heritage Lottery Fund (HLF), the Genealogical Society of Utah (GSU) and the National Archives of Scotland (NAS). SCAN aims to use the Internet to open up access to the contents of Scotland's archives through its website, *www.scan.org.uk*. This provides much useful information to a wide variety of sites and is a convenient gateway for genealogists and other historians. Fifty-two of Scotland's archives are partners in SCAN, and are in the process of compiling summary descriptions of individual collections held in many of the Scottish archives. In addition to these collection descriptions, SCAN has compiled a valuable Knowledge Base on all aspects of Scottish history. Unexpected delights to be discovered on the SCAN site include: a glossary of legal terms found in Scottish records; a currency converter for calculating modern equivalents of pre-decimal British money and pre-1707 Scottish currency; and a gazetteer of Scottish 'problem places'. The latter coaches the apprentice family historian to think in terms of the old administrative units of counties, parishes and burghs.

Scottish public registers, census records and wills

3.6   The official government source of genealogical data for Scotland is *www.scotlandspeople.gov.uk*. The General Register Office for Scotland (GROS), the NAS, SCAN and the Court of the Lord Lyon are partners in the ScotlandsPeople project, a major arm of the developing Scottish Family History Service. The site is already one of the world's biggest genealogical resources. Work is far advanced in giving Internet access to GROS's growing databases of indexes and images, covering the Scottish old parish registers (OPRs), statutory registers of births, marriages and deaths and census returns (up to 1901). For a full description of these services see Chapter 4. Visit *www.scotlandspeople.gov.uk* for news of developments and see also *www.gro-scotland.gov.uk*.

3.7   Under the auspices of SCAN, in agreement with the NAS, a searchable index of Scottish wills and testaments, presently up to 1901, is available online, with colour images of documents available to buy, save and download (*www.scottishdocuments.com*). A link to the Scottish wills site is also provided by *www.scan.org.uk*. For fuller information see Chapter 8.

Other government records and court and private records held by the NAS

3.8   The major initiative at the National Archives of Scotland is its online catalogue, a developing resource located on the website *www.nas.gov.uk*. It is a descriptive catalogue of NAS collections and as such covers the whole range of what we hold, other than material that has still to be catalogued. A significant part of what is in the catalogue is not of direct relevance to the family historian. Nevertheless it is a most important tool, covering as it does the records described in the following chapters. Used in combination with the information gleaned from those, the catalogue may help you identify NAS references for sets of records, or in many cases the call-up references of individual items or files. Some records are described in the briefest of terms, while in other cases fuller information about the contents of single documents or of series is found. Detailed information extracted from criminal trial records is included in the catalogue (see 14.2). The catalogue does not take you into images of the records themselves, so, as discussed in 3.3., you may well need to follow up on what you have found online.

National Library of Scotland

3.9   The range of the NLS's online manuscript catalogue is at time of writing limited. However the NLS has several databases available online dealing with the activities of Scots abroad. One is an important database of emigrants' correspondence and papers, and contains other material relating to emigration, all from manuscript collections of the NLS. For the most part this database gives brief catalogue descriptions. See *www.nls.uk/sitemap/databases.html*.

Public registers, census and government records held in England, Wales and Northern Ireland

3.10   These may be of relevance if you are searching for ancestors who have moved to or from Scotland, even temporarily, and therefore may be recorded in the registers of births, deaths and marriages, and census returns, outside Scotland. Such records also relate to government and public bodies whose holdings are of relevance to the whole of the United Kingdom.

The Family Records Centre (FRC), London

3.11 The FRC (*www.statistics.gov.uk/registration/family_records.asp*) does not offer Internet searching of its indexes or records. However, a visit to the Family Records Centre website is well worth making to discover more about their holdings and for the guidance given on records held elsewhere. Core resources held at the Centre are the indexes to records of births, deaths and marriages for England and Wales from 1837 and census returns 1841–1891. The BDM registers are not open to public inspection, but entries can be bought in the form of certificates. Other records held include microfilm of registered wills and administrations proved in the Prerogative Court of Canterbury, 1384–1858. The 1901 census for England and Wales is available online at *www.census.pro.gov.uk*

3.12 On the website of The National Archives (formerly the Public Record Office), the entry page to catalogues online at *www.pro.gov.uk/catalogues/default.htm* takes you into its own vast online catalogue, PROCAT. The National Archives' series of information leaflets has been incorporated into this. The same site also leads you into the A2A (Access to Archives) database, containing a number of catalogues submitted by archives in England. A2A's database of hospital records gives information on the existence and location of records of hospitals in the UK, but does not reproduce the catalogues in detail.

3.13 The Public Record Office of Northern Ireland (PRONI) is the main source for family history records in Northern Ireland and is the official place of deposit for all public records there. For information see *www.familyrecords.gov.uk*. Unfortunately almost no nineteenth-century Irish census returns survive, although census returns are available for 1901. RASCAL (Research And Special Collections Available Locally) is a gateway to research resources in libraries, museums and archives in Northern Ireland – *www.rascal.ac.uk*. The General Register Office (Northern Ireland) – *www.groni.gov.uk* – has an online service for birth and death certificates from 1864 and marriages from 1845.

3.14 *FamilyRecords.gov.uk* is a point of access to the partners in the *FamilyRecords.gov.uk* consortium, the aim being 'to help find the government records and other sources you need for your family history research'.

The partners are: A2A; British Library–India Office Records; Commonwealth War Graves Commission; Family Records Centre; General Register Office; General Register Office for Scotland; Imperial War Museum; Llyfrgell Genedlaethol Cymru/National Library Wales; The National Archives; National Archives of Scotland; Public Record Office of Northern Ireland; Scottish Archive Network. Also on this site there are many links to other sites of interest to the family historian, for example 'a glossary of archaic terms, as well as a number of modern Scots words and phrases, useful for genealogical research'.

The Republic of Ireland

3.15 If you are searching for ancestors who lived in the Republic of Ireland, visit the National Archives of Ireland at *www.nationalarchives.ie/index.html* and the General Register Office for Ireland at *www.groireland.ie*.

Other archives, libraries and local research centres

3.16 The Scottish Archive Network, through its directory at *www.scan.org.uk/directory*, gives contact information on partners in the Network and many others, including links to websites. Familia – *www.familia.org.uk* – is an essential guide to genealogical resources in public libraries in the UK and Ireland. Other gateways directing you to websites and services in the different parts of Scotland include *www.cyndislist.com* and *www.genuki.org.uk*. The gateway to descriptions of archive collections held by UK universities and colleges is the Archives Hub – *www.archiveshub.ac.uk*. In the main, collections are described only briefly on the Hub, but where possible there are links to complete catalogue descriptions. A splendid search tool is provided by the Hub for you to explore its indexes of subjects, place names, personal and corporate names. This quickly reveals the diversity of university and college archives, including much relating to the country's industrial and commercial heritage.

3.17 The range of help offered online to genealogists by archives, libraries and others serving different parts of Scotland and different specialist interests varies widely. On the one hand you may find genealogy research services as offered by the Angus Local Studies Centre, which specialises in researching Angus ancestors and can be commissioned to do this – *www.angus.gov.uk/history/default.htm*. On the other hand some hard-pressed organisations may offer you no more than an email address to write to. When you email them, in some cases you may receive only a leaflet or a standard response. It is likely in such circumstances that detailed work cannot be done in looking into records for you. The best advice about emails is to keep them brief, focussing on one or two precise points of real importance to you, which will give you the best chance of getting good advice back.

Other large genealogy websites

3.18 The Family History Library of the Church of Jesus Christ of Latter-day Saints has the largest collection of genealogical materials in the world. These include copies of a good proportion of the records referred to in 3.5-6. Go to *www.familysearch.org* or visit your local LDS family history centre to get access to the resources of this genealogical service. *Ancestry.com* is another Internet giant. It provides a subscription service for access to a huge collection of genealogical data. The large free genealogy site *RootsWeb.com* is one of its associates in the MyFamily.com, Inc. network.

Family and local history societies

3.19 There has been real benefit to Scottish culture in the gathering together and preservation of records and other evidence from the country's past and, best of all, information about ordinary people, by genealogists and local historians. One example of this is in the wealth of information held by the Scottish Genealogy Society – *www.scotsgenealogy.com* – in its Library and Family History Centre. Another is the enterprises of the Aberdeen & N.E. Scotland Family History Society, such as its growing list of transcriptions of north-east Scotland graveyards – *www.anesfhs.org.uk*. A third is the Glasgow & West of Scotland Family History Society's large projects, including co-operative ventures such as the indexing of poor law records for Glasgow, Lanarkshire and Dumbartonshire – see *www.gwsfhs.org.uk* and *www.glasgowlibraries.org*. For links to other family history societies see the website of the Scottish Association of Family History Societies – *www.safhs.org.uk* – or *www.genuki.org.uk* and *www.cyndislist.com*.

Clan societies and associations

3.20 Clan links are not usually the most useful ones with which to start family history research. Clan genealogies found in print, in manuscripts and on the web often relate to the grander families in the clan and shared family names of clan members do not mean that the latter are related, though some can well be. However membership of societies or associations may lead to the discovery of rewarding information and contacts. In that respect it helps that particular clan names are locally common in relatively small areas of the Highlands and Islands. It is also beneficial that many societies have active membership or fellow societies in other countries where Scots have settled. Such is the case, for example, with the great Clan Chattan (pronounced 'Hattan') confederation, with its constituent clans and many septs – see *www.clanchattan.org.uk*, which acts as a gateway to these. Other sites carrying links to Scottish clan societies include Electric Scotland – *www.scotsearch.org* – and *www.scotlandsclans.com*. There is also a good list in *http://clan-maccallum-malcolm.3acres.org/ScotClanFamily.html*. The webpage of the Library, Study and Genealogy Centre, at the Clan Donald Centre at Armadale on the Isle of Skye – *www.highlandconnection.org/cdltstudy.html* – is instructive. The Centre, which assists people to research West Highland ancestry, and not just Macdonald ancestry, is an example of what can be achieved when clan enthusiasm is part of the effort deployed.

Emigrants from Scotland

3.21 A salutary exercise when setting out to search for records of emigrants will be to have a look at the very fine work of the Immigrant Ships Transcribers' Guild (*www.immigrantships.org*). It can be dispiriting to find that there is often not enough information recorded in the lists to identify your ancestors with certainty. A gem to be found on the Scottish Archive Network's site is a searchable index of passenger lists, 1852-57, of the Highlands and Islands Emigration Society – *www.scan.org.uk/researchrtools/emigration.htm*. In those years the Society, which was set up to relieve destitution after the potato famine, assisted almost 5,000 people from western Scotland to emigrate to Australia. The SCAN 'knowledge base' entries on emigration, passenger lists and passports give sensible practical advice. *Ancestry.com* includes immigration and emigration databases. For another interesting source see details of the NLS databases at 3.9. Online searching and guidance would certainly have to be supplemented by referring to the passenger lists and emigration records that have been published in books, particularly in recent years.

Immigrants to the UK

3.22 For a useful introduction to this subject, see: *www.familyrecords.gov.uk/topics/immigration_1.htm*.

Occupations and social groups

3.23   One of the biggest challenges on the Internet is to track down records for occupational and social groups, such as paupers, prisoners, fishwives, members of craft incorporations and guilds, soldiers, handloom weavers, miners and steelworkers. Searches of online catalogues are an obvious option. Visits to the websites with relevant local and social interests – see 3.16, 3.17 and 3.20 – would be a priority. It is of course always worth checking for links using the big gateways mentioned above, including those which *www.genuki.org.uk* gives to sources on 'United Kingdom and Ireland occupations'. On a variety of websites military records figure quite highly among the occupation groups considered. The Scottish Archive Network's 'knowledge base', see 3.16, a database of answers to questions frequently asked in Scottish archives, combined with a directory of where to find historical records, suggests there is some demand for help in finding records dealing with different classes of people. Advice is provided on topics including poor relief, policemen, school admission registers and log books, scholars, prisoners and suffragettes.

3.24   The following chapters will not answer all the questions you have about your ancestors. But the richness and variety of what is described in this book is something that is not yet generally found on the web. In other words the latter has some way to go before it fully serves the purposes that books do now.

∾ 4 ∾

The General Register Office for Scotland
(The Registrar-General's Department)
by Martin Tyson

4.1   Under the direction of the Registrar General for Scotland, the General Register Office for Scotland (GROS), a Government department, administers the registration of births, deaths and marriages. The Registrar General is also responsible for the taking of decennial censuses of the population of Scotland. The GROS is located in New Register House in Edinburgh, conveniently situated for family historians next door to the NAS's main building, General Register House.

4.2   For people interested in doing their family history, various leaflets are available from the GROS and are updated each year: *A List of the Main Records in the Care of the Registrar General*; *Searching by Our Staff for a Particular Event*; and *Guidance for General Search Customers in New Register House*. You can obtain copies by calling in person or writing, faxing or telephoning New Register House, Edinburgh EHI 3YT (telephone: 0131–334 0380; fax: 0131–314 4400; international code +44131). Full texts of the leaflets, and further information about GROS, are available online at: *www.gro-scotland.gov.uk*.

4.3   Through the same telephone numbers (or 0131–314 4449 or 4450) you may reserve one of the limited number of search-room seats available for advance booking, or make use of a discounted advance-purchase pass (Apex) when available. While it is not necessary to book in advance, you are advised to do so if travelling any distance to Edinburgh, as there is a great demand for seats, particularly during the summer months. A place booked for a particular day will be held for you until 10:00, but if you fail to appear or do not call to say that you have been delayed, the place may be let to someone else. Alternatively, you can simply come to New Register House without a booking, as many of our search places are filled on a 'first-come, first-served' basis.

4.4 Booking a place is free, but you will need to buy a valid pass to search the records. You can buy a search pass for a day; a week; four weeks; a quarter or a year. A part-day search pass is also available, but only after 13:00, and no advance bookings for part-day searches can be made. Paying the statutory fee for a search pass gives you the right to search in the indexes to the post-1855 statutory registers of births, deaths and marriages; the pre-1855 old parish registers (OPRs); and the open census returns 1841 to 1901. You also have a right to buy an extract; that is, an authenticated copy of any individual register entry.

4.5 In addition, at the discretion of the Registrar General, those who have paid the fee are also permitted to look at copies of the actual entries in the registers of births, deaths and marriages etc. identified from the indexes, and to take notes. As a result of the Digital Imaging of the Genealogical Records of Scotland's people (DIGROS) project, these copies are increasingly in the form of digital images of the record pages, linked to the individual index entries. For records where the DIGROS process has not been completed, copies will be in the form of microfilm and microfiche.

4.6 New Register House is open Mondays to Fridays (except public holidays) between the hours of 09:00 and 16:30. Access to the records is not allowed to anyone under the age of 12. Children of 12 or 13 may be allowed access, but only if accompanied by their parent or legal guardian. Children aged 14 to 16 may be allowed access unaccompanied provided they can show written parental or guardian consent to their searching the records. Normal fees are payable in all cases. Tell the staff in advance if you have any disability which might make it difficult for you to use the search facilities. A search in the GROS involves, for example, moving around the building, opening filing-cabinet drawers of various heights, and viewing a computer screen and microfiche reader. If you have difficulty doing this, free admission may be given to someone assisting you.

4.7 On arrival you will be issued with a numbered ticket and directed through to a waiting-room. If you have already paid in advance for an Apex pass, ask as you come in and you can collect it without waiting. When it is your turn to be served your number will be displayed, and you should go through to the nearby public counter where the staff will discuss with you the kind of search you wish to do, and ask you for the appropriate fee. They will issue you with a search pass and a seat number, and direct you to the appropriate search room where your numbered seat is located. There are four search rooms in New Register House with a total of just over 100 search places. The pass for New Register House is personal and not normally transferable to anyone else, though special rules apply to one-year passes.

4.8 The supervisor in the search room will give you a short introduction on how to use the facilities. Your searching will involve the DIGROS computer system, using indexes to call up digital images of records; computer indexes, microfiche and microfilm readers; the location of the fiche and film; and of the finding aids and reference books, which are easy to use.

4.9 Most GROS records are now available through the DIGROS computer system. You access this by inputting your name and seat number, and then selecting the type of record you wish to search, whether statutory births, deaths, marriages, census returns or other types of record. A simple search form will appear, asking you to input the name of the person you are looking for, together with other details if known. Once you enter this, a list of index entries fitting the criteria you have chosen will appear. You then select the item you are interested in by clicking on the person's name. A digitised image of the register or record page containing that person's entry will appear, from which you can take notes, or of which (within certain date limits) you can obtain an inexpensive unofficial print-out by clicking the printer button. Where DIGROS images are not completed, records are available by means of self-service access on microfiche or microfilm. You can withdraw a fiche or film from the self-service areas by completing the appropriate order-slip. Insert the completed order-slip in place of the fiche or film you wish to look at, and take it back to the reader equipment located on your desk. You can take out up to three microfiche or two microfilm reels at any one time. When you have finished with any records, you simply leave it in the appropriate tray for re-filing by the staff. Search-room staff are available to give guidance, but not to conduct searches for you.

4.10 To protect the valuable records, you will not be permitted to smoke, eat or drink anywhere in New Register House, including the toilet areas. There are many cafes, pubs, restaurants and sandwich-bars within easy walking distance.

4.11 For those unable to visit New Register House to research their family history, ScotlandsPeople, GROS's private sector partners, run a pay–per–view website (*http://www.scotlandspeople.gov.uk*) on its behalf, which gives access to some of the indexes and digital images available at New Register House. The site provides a free search to give you some indication of how many entries you will find on the site for a particular name. However, to search further, you will need to pay an access fee (by credit card, through a secure payment mechanism) which will give you a certain number of 'credits', allowing you to download a given number of index entries or digital images. The site contains indexes and images of statutory registers of births up to 100 years ago, marriages up to 75 years ago and deaths up to 50 years ago. It also has indexes and images for the 1891 and 1901 censuses; indexes to the 1881 census; and indexes to the Old Parish Register baptisms and births and proclamations of banns and marriages. More digital image material will be added as it becomes available. Having downloaded index entries or images to your own PC you are welcome to print or save them for personal use. You are also able to order official extract certificates of entries of records you have found in the indexes direct from the site (again, payment is by credit card).

Births, Deaths and Marriages since 1855

4.12 In Scotland compulsory civil registration of births, deaths and marriages began on 1 January 1855 under the Registration of Births, Deaths and Marriages (Scotland) Act 1854. Tracing a line of descent back to 1855 can be a fairly straightforward task provided you start with some good details about more recent members of your family. The GROS holds a complete set of the statutory registers comprising all the births, deaths and marriages registered since 1855 in all the registration districts in Scotland, originally 1027 in number. It is likely that you will want to start your family search in these registers, unless your ancestors left Scotland before 1855.

4.13 Within a few weeks of any birth, death or marriage being registered in Scotland, the event is added to the appropriate computer index, and simple step-by-step instructions are provided for working the easy-to-use computer terminals in the search rooms. All events registered since 1855 can now be looked up on the computer, but the computer indexes were in the main prepared from paper indexes compiled at the time, so their contents vary.

4.14 The *birth indexes* give details of the child's name; the year of registration;

registration district name and number; and register entry number. From 1929 onwards the mother's maiden surname is also given.

4.15 The *death indexes* give the deceased's name; age at death; the year of registration; registration district name and number; and register entry number. From 1855 to 1865 the age at death was not recorded in the old paper indexes, but these ages are gradually being added to the computer indexes. Separate entries exist for both female married names and maiden names. From 1974, the mother's surname is included for both male and female deaths. Ages given by informants may be only approximate, particularly in the early decades of registration, and in the cases of persons born before compulsory civil registration began.

4.16 The *marriage indexes* give each party's name; the year of registration; registration district name and number; and register entry number. From 1929 onwards, the spouse's surname is also given.

4.17 There are a number of points to note about the indexes. First, the spelling of names may be unusual, particularly during the earlier period of registration. The indexes record the names as spelt by the registrar at the time, irrespective of present-day spelling. To help overcome these variations, a Soundex facility has been incorporated into the indexes, and this can be used to identify alternative spellings or similar sounding surnames. Secondly, names beginning 'Mac' and 'Mc' are indexed separately. You should therefore check both if you have difficulty in finding the entry you are looking for. Once you have traced an entry you would like to see in the indexes, consult the register entry itself.

4.18 Entries in the statutory registers of births from 1861 include: name, date, time and place of birth; sex; father's name and profession; mother's name and maiden name; date and place of marriage; signature and qualification of informant, and residence if out of the house in which the birth occurred.

4.19 Entries in the registers of deaths from 1861 include: name; rank or profession; marital status; spouse's name; when and where died; sex; age; father's name and rank or profession; mother's name and maiden name; cause of death; signature and qualification of informant, and residence if out of the house in which the death occurred.

4.20 Entries in the register of marriages from 1861 include: when, where and how married (e.g. after banns, according to the forms of the Church of Scotland). For both bridegroom and bride are given: name; rank or profession; marital status; age; usual residence; father's name and rank or profession; mother's name and maiden name. In the case of regular marriages, names of the officiating minister (or registrar from 1940) and witnesses are recorded. In the case of irregular marriages, date of conviction (to 1939), decree of declarator, or sheriff's warrant is given.

4.21 You will find that there is some variation from the above in the information registered between 1855 and 1860. The first year of civil registration in Scotland, 1855, is particularly good, with fuller details recorded about individuals and their families. If you are lucky enough to find an ancestor who was born, died or married in this year, the additional information supplied can be very full indeed and may include some of the following details.

In the registers of births for 1855: name; whether informant present at birth; baptismal name (if different) or name given without baptism; sex; date, and time of birth; where born; father's name and rank, profession or occupation, age and birthplace; when and where married, and any previous issue, both living and deceased; mother's name and maiden name, how many children she has had, age and where born; signature and qualification of informant, and residence if out of the house where the birth occurred.

In the registers of deaths for 1855: name; rank, profession or occupation; sex; age; where born and how long in district; parents' names, and rank, profession or occupation; if married, spouse's name and names and ages of any children; date of death and time; where died; cause of death, length of illness, by whom certified and when they last saw the deceased; burial place, undertaker by whom certified: signature and qualification of informant.

In the registers of marriages for 1855: when, where and how married; (and, for both bridegroom and bride) signatures; present and usual residences; age; rank and profession; relationship of parties, if related; marital status; children by any previous marriages, whether living or dead; where parties were born; the date and place of registration of birth; parents' names, rank, profession or occupation; if a regular marriage, signatures of officiating minister and witnesses; if irregular, date of conviction or decree of declarator and court where pronounced.

4.22 Corrections or changes to the registered particulars – for example, in the cases of divorce or change of name – are recorded in the *Register of Corrected Entries,* or *Register of Corrections Etc.* The entries in the registers of births, deaths and marriages are cross-referenced to these.

4.23 The GROS also holds indexes for series of records of births, deaths and marriages which occurred outside Scotland, but which relate to Scots:

- Marine register of births and deaths (from 1855);
- Air register of births and deaths (from 1948);
- Service records (from 1881);
- War registers (from 1899);
- Consular returns of births, deaths and marriages (from 1914);
- High Commissioners' returns of births and deaths (from 1964);
- Registers of births, deaths and marriages in foreign countries (1860-1965);
- Foreign marriages (from 1947).

These records are in some cases patchy and incomplete. Further details about them are in the GROS leaflet, *List of main records in the care of the Registrar General.*

4.24 The statutory registers of births, deaths and marriages are all duplicated, with one copy held centrally in New Register House, as described, and a second copy held locally. There is some limited provision for searching the duplicate copies held by local registrars. Moreover, a number of local search centres now exist which contain copies of fiche for areas other than their own strict registration area. Some offices have online access to the computerised indexes at New Register House. With the advent of the DIGROS digital imaging project, it will become possible for local registration offices with the necessary communications links to give access to all the digital images and indexes (of census returns and Old Parish Registers, as well as statutory registers) available in New Register House. Before you visit a local registration office it is advisable to telephone first to ask about their facilities. As mentioned in 4.11 above, it is also possible to access some of the statutory registers online through the ScotlandsPeople website.

Births, Deaths and Marriages before 1855

4.25 If you have been lucky enough to get back beyond the year 1855, and have not come to a dead end during your search of the Scottish statutory registers – which may happen if, for example, your ancestors came to Scotland from Ireland – then the old parish registers (OPRs) may take you further back beyond this date. Many of these registers are available in the GROS, where those that survived were deposited under the Registration Act of 1854 to form a splendid continuity with the statutory registers.

4.26 The OPRs are the registers of the established church, the Church of Scotland, which record births and baptisms; proclamations of banns or marriages; and deaths or burials, up to 1854. The parish ministers or session clerks of some 900 parishes kept these registers until their formal transfer to the GROS. The surviving registers number approximately 3,500 but they are far from complete. Though the oldest register relates to baptisms and banns in 1553 for the parish of Errol in Perthshire, for some parishes the earliest registers date from the early nineteenth century, while for others there may be no registers at all. A lot of parishes do not have any burial or death registers. The standard of record-keeping varied considerably from parish to parish and from year to year, and most entries contain relatively little information in comparison to the statutory registers.

4.27 You should therefore set out with optimism tinged with realism when tackling the OPRs. Remember also that although registration in the Church of Scotland's registers was in theory compulsory for all denominations, it was both costly and unpopular. Members of other churches, such as the Free Church of Scotland or Roman Catholic Church, may not be recorded, though with luck you may be able to find some (see Chapter 7 for alternatives). Also, as populations shifted and cities started to develop in the nineteenth century, religion began to lose its hold, and as few as 30 per cent of events may be recorded for certain urban parishes.

4.28 There are computer indexes to all the registers of births and baptisms, and of banns and marriages. There are no computer indexes for the registers of deaths or burials, but paper indexes exist for a few of them. Lists of the indexed material are available in each of the search rooms. The OPRs have been added to the Genealogical Society of Utah's International Genealogical Index (IGI) and to its FamilySearch family history software, which is also available for reference in New Register House.

4.29 The OPR computerised indexes contain some seven million birth, baptism and marriage entries. You can search either the whole of Scotland for a particular name, or just a specific county and decade, for example Perthshire for 1800-1809. As with the statutory registers, the index entries are being linked to digital images of the register pages as part of the DIGROS project, and the images, as well as the indexes, will eventually be available on the ScotlandsPeople website.

4.30 The *births and baptism indexes* give details of the child's name; parents' names; date of birth or baptism; and the reference number and name of the parish where the baptism took place.

4.31 The *banns and marriages indexes* give the name of the person who was married; the name of their spouse; date of proclamation or marriage; and the reference number and name of the parish where the marriage took place.

4.32 The GROS has a catalogue of the OPRs arranged alphabetically by parish name within counties. This gives details of the dates covered for each type of event, and the reference numbers allocated to each register. If you have the name of a place but do not know what parish it is in, there is a collection of directories, gazetteers and maps in the New Register House Library to assist you. To preserve the original OPR volumes from overuse, consultation of the registers is from microfilm and, shortly, digital images, not the originals.

4.33 There are no hard and fast rules about the details given in the OPR pages themselves. These vary from parish to parish, and the information can be very thin. In the case of baptisms, aside from the name of the child and the date of the baptism, you might hope to obtain the names of both parents, their place or parish of residence, and perhaps the occupation of the father. On some occasions a list of witnesses may be supplied. For marriages, you might expect to find the date on which the marriage took place or was contracted, the names of the parties and their place or parishes of residence. If you are lucky enough to have an ancestor with a relatively uncommon surname, this can be useful when attempting to identify the correct entry from the indexes. Unfortunately, remote parishes such as those in the Highlands are notoriously difficult, with the same combinations of forenames and surnames common to particular localities. These names may crop up again and again, for example, John Mackay; Kenneth Mackenzie; Mary Macdonald; Ann Ross; Margaret Fraser.

Census Records (1841–1891)

4.34 Census records can make an excellent bonus for the family historian who visits New Register House. They can both fill out information about families already traced in the registers of births, deaths and marriages and other sources, and lead you to ancestors or family members whom you had not previously identified.

4.35 The Registrar General holds records of the decennial census of the population of Scotland for 1841 and every tenth year thereafter (with the exception of the wartime year of 1941 when no census was taken). The records of censuses taken after 1901 are still confidential and are not available for searching or extracting until 100 years after the date of each census. Census records open to the public relate to the censuses held on 7 June 1841; 31 March 1851; 8 April 1861; 3 April 1871; 4 April 1881, 5 April 1891 and 31 March 1901. These records are transcript books prepared by the census enumerators after the census schedules were collected from individual households within each parish.

4.36 The census books generally contain particulars such as name; age; sex; marital status; relationship to head of the household; occupation and birthplace of every member of a household present at that address on census night, including servants, lodgers and visitors. However, details do vary from census year to census year. It is worth bearing in mind that nineteenth-century households could include many people who were not actually part of the family as such, including servants or apprentices. Also, places such as hotels and lodging houses counted as one household, and if the person for whom you are searching was staying at an hotel on census night, he or she will be recorded with this 'household' rather than with their family, as you might be expecting. Institutions such as prisons, workhouses and hospitals were enumerated separately from other households in their area.

4.37 The returns for the 1841 census year are the least detailed. Marital status and relationship to head of the household was not recorded. Birthplace details confirm only if an individual was born within the Scottish county being enumerated or not. If the person was born outwith that county, unfortunately no other county name is given and, if born furth of Scotland, only the initial letter of the country of birth is given: for example, 'E' for England; 'I' for Ireland; 'F' for France. Also, the ages given may not always be accurate. In Some cases enumerators may have recorded the actual age given, but they were instructed to round down ages for persons over the age of 15. Thus, persons between the ages of 15 and 20 can have age recorded as 15; between 20 and 25, recorded as 20; between 25 and 30 recorded as 25, etc.

4.38 By the year 1851, marital status; relationship to head of the household; and fuller details of birthplace, including place and county of birth, were added. Details of whether a person was blind or deaf and dumb are also noted. By 1861, additional details such as number of children attending school, and numbers of rooms with one or more windows, are also recorded, as from 1891 was the fact of a person being a Gaelic speaker. These will help you to build a more detailed picture of your ancestors, their family circumstances and the accommodation in which they lived.

4.39 The entries in the census books were not indexed by the enumerators, and in order to trace any particular household in the 1841-71 censuses one needs to have some knowledge of the address they were at when the census was taken. Street indexes are available for certain large urban areas and the bigger towns. These identify the census books for each small 'enumeration district' in which addresses are recorded, and are invaluable particularly for the cities, which cover many books. At the front of each enumeration book you will find a short description of the area it covers. Add to this the difficulty of different parts of streets often being included in several enumeration districts, and the tedium of looking through, for example, the city of Glasgow census returns without street indexes can be imagined. When searching census records, therefore, you should start out with enough information to identify positively the person or family you are looking for, including their town or parish of residence. For people living in large towns, it greatly helps to know their exact address.

The GROS holds catalogues from which you can identify the census districts and the reference numbers for these. For the census years 1841 and 1851, the districts are arranged alphabetically within counties. For later censuses they are simply arranged alphabetically.

4.40 The GROS has also made available computerised indexes of all the names enumerated for the census years 1881, 1891 and 1901. They consist of over three million entries for each census year and will permit you to search these records more easily.

4.41 The 1881 census index consists of a full set of all the information contained in the enumerators' transcript books. You can search this index and dis-cover complete details of the enumerated entries for each household, and the specific details for each individual within that household. In theory, therefore, it is not necessary to inspect the original census record, though we would always recommend that you do so in order to satisfy yourself that you have obtained the correct census information.

4.42 The 1891 and 1901 census indexes on DIGROS consist of index entries only, similar to the indexes for the statutory registers and OPRs. The 1891 and 1901 indexes gives details of name; sex; age; name and number of the registration district and enumeration district; and page number of the census entry. Through the DIGROS system (or online through the ScotlandsPeople website), it is then possible to access directly a digital image of the enumeration book.

4.43 In addition to these indexes, certain privately produced indexes for other census years and specific counties or parishes are available and these are continually being added to. They are far from being a complete coverage of all the census data, but they may be of possible use if your ancestors came from particular areas. Details of these are available in the search rooms.

4.44 Consultation of the census records is increasingly through digital images on the DIGROS system. Where imaging has not been completed, records are consulted from microfilm. Copies of these and the OPR microfilms are sold to libraries and other institutions throughout the world. It is there-fore possible to inspect many of these films in places other than the GROS.

∞ 5 ∞

The Court of the Lord Lyon

5.1 The Court of the Lord Lyon is situated in New Register House, alongside the General Register Office for Scotland. If your ancestors were members of the nobility or large landowners you may have cause to use their services. The Court of the Lord Lyon is responsible for the administration of the system of heraldry in Scotland which has evolved into a precise science. The Public Register of All Arms and Bearings in Scotland, established in 1672, the Public Register of Genealogies and Birthbrieves in Scotland, and considerable genealogical material is in the custody of the Court of the Lord Lyon, which also maintains a large private library. The

New Register House

31

staff of the Court of the Lord Lyon do not undertake genealogical research, and requests for specific searches in the Public Registers attract a
search fee.

5.2   Heraldry, although allied to family research, is a fascinating and specialised
field in its own right, much of it outside the scope of this book. For more
information you may contact the Heraldry Society of Scotland through
their web site at *www.heraldry-scotland.co.uk*. Enquiries regarding genealogical materials held in the Court of the Lord Lyon should be made in
writing to: The Lyon Clerk, Court of the Lord Lyon, HM New Register
House, Edinburgh, EH1 3YT.

∞ 6 ∞

At the National Archives of Scotland

6.1 You are now ready to visit the National Archives of Scotland. Try to be clear in your mind what information you are seeking and what records you want to see. Before your visit, especially if you do not live in Edinburgh, please contact us to find out where and whether the records you want to see may be consulted. This will also enable us to inform you if records are unavailable, perhaps because they are on exhibition or undergoing conservation treatment. This is most important to prevent you from making a wasted journey, particularly if you are travelling from a distance. Records may be in General Register House or West Register House or in a local record office elsewhere in Scotland (see Appendix A). Some records are stored in a building in the suburbs of Edinburgh and consequently a day's notice will be required before you can see such records in a search room. As records are sometimes transferred from one location to another, the present location of most of the records is not specified in this book. However, you will probably go first to General Register House, as the records currently held there include the legal registers, wills and church records. Please also give advance notice if you are disabled. Seats in the Search Rooms are not bookable in advance.

6.2 When you arrive at General (or West) Register House, tell the duty staff that you have come to do research in the Historical (or West) Search Room, and they will direct you there. On your first visit, you will have to complete a visitor's form. Remember to bring a pencil with you every time, as ink in any form is banned from the search rooms (in case of accidental damage to the records). Bring notepaper. On your first visit, bring a means of identification such as driving licence, passport, bank or credit card or other evidence of address. You will be asked to leave your outer garments and bag in a cloakroom. Remember to take your identification, pencil and notebook with you.

6.3 You have arrived in one of the search rooms on your first visit to the

NAS. A member of staff will speak to you, issue you with a reader's ticket and a copy of the search room regulations, show you where the catalogues and indexes are kept, and give such preliminary advice as is required. Your reader's ticket will be valid for up to three years. Keep it carefully, as you will need to bring it on subsequent visits to gain admittance to the search rooms. It entitles you to see the records without charge. You will be asked to hand it over every time you order out any records.

6.4   Though staff are on hand to advise you further and to answer reasonable questions, you will be the person carrying out the research. The records are divided into various groups, listed in a Summary Catalogue of all the records. Each record group has its own reference code, consisting of letters (e.g. AD, CC, E, GD). Each document has its own unique reference (or call) number, consisting of a group code followed by a series of numbers (e.g. AD14/53/203). The guides to the records take various forms and some are easier to use or more thorough than others. Each group of records has its own catalogue which supplies the date, description and reference number of each document or set of documents. There are indexes to some collections, but many records are not indexed. Perhaps a quick word of explanation on the difference between a catalogue and an index would be helpful: a catalogue is a descriptive list of records, containing entries such as 'Letter from Sir Walter Scott to the Lady of the Lake' whereas an index is an alphabetical list of names, places etc referring to catalogue entries eg 'Scott, Sir Walter, letter from, to the Lady of the Lake, GD999/1'. Also available are source lists that gather together records from various groups relating to particular subjects, e.g. Canada, Coal Mining, Military records. These were compiled some years ago, before the advent of computer cataloguing. As such, they have been partly superseded but they can still prove useful if you are researching a particular subject.

6.5   The National Archives of Scotland has recently made its catalogues available electronically, both in the search rooms and online (*www.nas.gov.uk*). In consequence, some of the advice on searching the records which follows below may be short-circuited by a search of the electronic catalogue. However, the procedures for searching have been described in detail since the electronic catalogue may not always carry specific information on every item in a series of records. In addition, some readers still prefer to search paper catalogues where these are available, and there may be times when the electronic catalogue is off-line for maintenance or updating.

6.6   Whenever a group of records or series of documents or individual document is mentioned in this book, its reference number will be given in brackets, eg GD1/99. You may find it helpful as you go through this book to note down the references of records classes which sound promising.

6.7   To see a document, order it by means of an order slip on which you write its reference number (or 'call number'), your name, the date, and the number of your seat in the search room. You must write a separate slip for each reference number. You may usually order a maximum of three at one time. If your research requires you to see more than three items at any one time, please speak to the search room staff.

Please use BLOCK CAPITALS and write in PENCIL	ORDER SLIP A separate slip must be completed for each item required. For a printed book, please state reference, author, title and number of volumes.	FOR OFFICIAL USE		
		LEGAL		
		HIST.		
REFERENCE OR DESCRIPTION		KEEP OUT		
		PHOTOST.	KEPT OUT	
CH3/214/1		MICROF.		
		REPAIR		
		STAFF	REPLACED DATE / INITIALS	
		RETRANS.		
READER'S NAME A. READER	DATE 21/10/03 SEAT No. 13	No. OF PIECES		

Order slip used in Historical and West Search Rooms

6.8   Most of the catalogues will have an introductory note explaining the background and content of the collection along with a more detailed contents list. If there is no contents list, see if the Summary Catalogue supplies this defect. Modern catalogues are compiled to a common form, with the reference numbers in the left-hand margin.

6.9   Indexes vary tremendously in quality and style. Pre-twentieth century manuscript 'indexes' may not be indexes in our understanding of the word, sometimes being a contents list, and sometimes alphabetical only as far as the first letter of each surname.

6.10 Surnames beginning with 'Mc' or 'Mac' may be indexed as if 'Mc' (or 'Mac') was a separate letter of the alphabet or may be combined with the letter 'M' in the English fashion. On very rare occasions, they may be indexed by the letter following the 'Mc', i.e. 'Macdonald' would be found under the letter 'D' (e.g. in LC9/3/1).

Reference	
CH2/700	**New Luce Kirk Session 1694-1995**
CH2/700/1	Minutes 1694-1741 Contribution for bell and steeple 1730 1694-1741
CH2/700/2	Minutes 1725-1770 (Perhaps scroll)
CH2/700/3	Minutes 1742-70 Minutes 1803-21 Accounts 1803-26 (poors' fund) 1742-1826
CH2/700/4	Minutes 1788-1803 (Scroll)
CH2/700/5	Minutes 1822-1855
CH2/700/6	Minutes 1855-1893
CH2/700/7	Poors' fund accounts 1826-47 Parish Board minutes 1847-66 1826-1866
CH2/700/8	Accounts 1874-1897
CH2/700/9	Baptismal register 1855-1954
CH2/700/10	Marriage register 1855-1971
CH2/700/11	Proclamation register 1855-1977
CH2/700/12	Communion roll 1855-1927
CH2/700/13	Kirk session minutes 1894-1995
GB/234/CH2/700	New Luce Kirk Session 1694-1977 Minutes, 1694-1770 and 1788-1893; Contribution for bell and steeple, 1730; Poor's fund accounts, 1803-1847; Parish Board minutes, 1847-1866; Accounts, 1874-1897; Baptismal register, 1855-1954; Marriage register, 1855-1971; Proclamation register, 1855-1977; Communion roll, 1855-1927.

National Archives of Scotland   Created on 23/05/03

Page in an NAS catalogue.

6.11 'Mc' means 'son of' and in the Highlands and Islands until the eighteenth century its appearance in a name might mean just that. Duncan Dow McEan VcEwen was the son of Ean (John) and grandson of Ewen (Dow being a nickname meaning 'black'). Duncan's son would probably bear the name 'McDonachie' or a variant thereof. Similarly, in the Northern Isles, particularly Shetland, Andrew Davidson could be the son of David Manson, who was the son of Magnus. It is difficult to specify a date when such 'patronymics' stuck as modern surnames.

6.12 In Scotland, a woman does not in a legal sense 'change her name' on marriage. Thus, married women are usually described in documents and indexed under their maiden name or, more recently, with alternative surnames (eg Mary Stewart, wife of William Sim; Mary Stewart or Sim).

6.13 In the older catalogues and indexes, two types of numerals may be used: roman numbers (i, ii, iii, iv etc) and our conventional arabic numbers (1, 2, 3, 4 etc). If these numbers are part of a reference or call number, convert a roman number into an arabic number, when ordering out or referring to a document.

6.14 Some older catalogues give surnames and place-names as they are spelled in the document. Current practice is to provide the modern form of the name, with the original version in brackets. Some indexes modernise names, some do not. Look under all possible variants of the surname you are seeking.

6.15 Most catalogues and indexes give not only the forename(s) and surname of each individual but also his 'designation'. This designation may include his occupation, where he lives, or a relationship, usually the name and designation of his father: eg John Fulton, bonnet-maker in Kilmarnock, George Duncan, son of John D., portioner of Auchtermuchty ('portioner' means he owned part of these lands).

6.16 Some of the more important records are public registers, which may consist not only of volumes, but also of 'warrants'. A warrant is the authority for certain information to be put into the register. Sometimes the warrant is an original document, sometimes signed, that has been copied into a volume of the register.

6.17 You will soon become accustomed to variant and eccentric spellings in the documents you read. Newcomers to research in Scottish documents will encounter two other particular problems. The first is that documents before the eighteenth century were written in unfamiliar scripts, with many letterforms different from those we use today. Learning to read these older scripts is not difficult, but does take practice. Useful books are *Scottish Handwriting 1150–1650* by Grant G Simpson (Tuckwell Press) and *Scottish Handwriting 1500–1700: a self-help pack* by Alison Rosie (Scottish Record Office and Scottish Records Association, 1994). If you live in or near Edinburgh, you might like to attend an evening class on Scottish Handwriting held in General Register House each winter under the auspices of Edinburgh University.

6.18 The second problem is the language in which documents are written. Until recently, many Scottish documents were written in Scots, a form of English with its own vocabulary and phraseology. This is where a dictionary becomes invaluable. More awkwardly, until well on in the nineteenth century, important legal documents were in Latin. However, a very small knowledge of Latin and some practice in recognising the salient parts of such documents can help considerably. In post-medieval Latin documents, surnames and place-names are mostly in Scots and English.

6.19 In subsequent chapters, advice is given on how to search relevant groups of records. There is one group of records that appears in most chapters and therefore it is convenient to describe it here. That group consists of records known as Gifts and Deposits (GD), which are the records of private individuals, families, organisations and business concerns, which have been gifted or are on loan to the NAS. They contain an infinite variety of records and information and often supplement other groups of records. Look at the index to the Summary Catalogue to see if they include a collection of papers in which you are interested and if there is a catalogue of that particular collection. A few of the GDs are also described in two published volumes, *List of Gifts and Deposits in the Scottish Record Office* (which may be bought from the NAS). Smaller GDs are referenced as GD1. Larger GDs each have their own reference number, eg the Earl of Airlie's records are GD16. Other collections of family and business papers may be found in local record offices (see Appendix A).

6.20 Of the GD collections, the most useful for you are probably those of the big landowning families, as the names of those who lived in their estates may appear among their estate papers. If you know the area where your ancestor lived, you may want to find out who were the landowners in that area. The parish reports printed in the *Old* and *New Statistical Accounts* *of Scotland* usually provide this information for the end of the eighteenth century and around 1840 respectively. These are also available online at *http://edina.ac.uk/stat-acc-scot/*. Another useful guide is *A Directory of land-ownership in Scotland c1770* edited by Loretta R. Timperley (Scottish Record Society).

6.21 There is also a series of private records referenced RH15. The titles of these collections are indexed both in the Summary Catalogue and in a separate RH15 index. RH is the reference number for a varied series of records of mixed and sometimes uncertain origin. They include transcripts and photocopies (RH2) and microfilms (RH4) of various records held elsewhere.

6.22 Copies of most documents may be bought, provided the format and condition of the records is suitable and there are no copyright or preservation restrictions. Searchroom staff can provide advice on all aspects of copying.

6.23 A small number of the records are closed to public access. These are a few GD collections which the owner has placed under restriction, collections which have not yet been catalogued, collections containing sensitive personal data, the disclosure of which would be likely to cause substantial damage or distress, and some recent government records.

6.24 Closure periods on government records can range from 30 to 100 years. It is possible to request access to closed government records and NAS search room staff can explain how to go about this if you need to do so. The system of closure periods will cease when the 2002 Freedom of Information (Scotland) Act comes into force on 1 January 2005. At that point, all information held by bodies covered under the Act – including all government information – will be open unless it falls under one of the exemptions to FOI listed in the Act. Some records, which are currently closed, are also likely to be exempt from the provisions of FOI, but it will still be possible to request access to them. Once the Act comes into force, NAS search room staff will be able to guide you through the procedures for this.

6.25 The National Register of Archives for Scotland, which is a branch of the NAS, surveys private records kept elsewhere in Scotland. An index to and copies of these surveys may be consulted in our searchrooms or through the electronic catalogue *www.nas.gov.uk*. If you want to consult documents mentioned in a survey, contact the secretary of the NRAS for further advice. However, papers that are still in private hands are often not available for genealogical research.

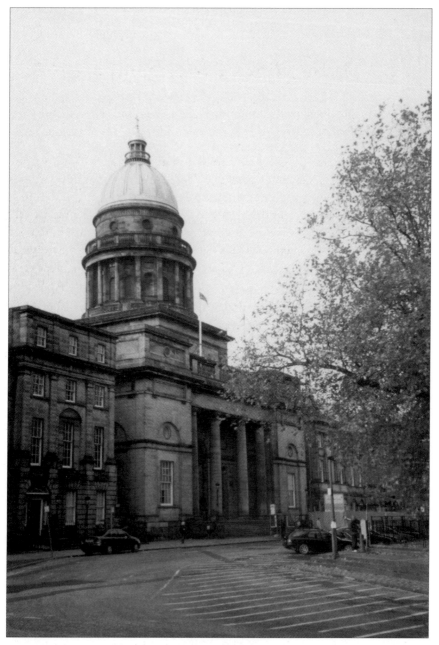

West Register House

∞ 7 ∞

Births, Baptisms, Marriages and Burials

7.1   If you are searching before statutory registration began in 1855, and cannot find a record of birth, marriage or death in the Old Parish Registers in New Register House, then you should look at the records in the NAS. Remember that Old Parish Registers were compiled by ministers of the Church of Scotland. Your ancestor may have been a member of one of the many other Presbyterian churches in Scotland, or an Episcopalian or Roman Catholic. It therefore helps considerably if you know the religious denomination of your ancestor, as well as the essential information of the approximate place of residence. *The Old Statistical Account* is a useful source of information as to which denominations were active in particular parishes at the end of the eighteenth century. The books listed in 18.1 record the locations of most of the Presbyterian (sometimes also called 'non-conformist') congregations which have existed in Scotland.

7.2   *If your ancestor was Protestant*, go to the catalogue labelled CH. The non-conformist records are numbered CH3 and CH10–16, of which the bulkiest are CH3, the records of the former free churches which have become re-united with the Church of Scotland. Other churches covered by these series are:

- Society of Friends or Quakers (CH10)
- Methodist (CH11)
- Episcopal (CH12)
- United Free Church (CH13)
- Congregational (CH14)
- Unitarian (CH15)
- Free Church (CH16)

For information on the complicated history of the various Presbyterian denominations in Scotland, look at Andrew Drummond and James

Bulloch's two books *The Scottish Church 1688-1843* and *The Church in Victorian Scotland, 1843-1874* (St Andrew Press).

Not all of the congregations of these churches have deposited their records in the National Archives of Scotland, but the NAS also has microfilm copies of Episcopal Church registers, arranged by diocese. These are listed in the RH4 catalogue at RH4/179-185 and appendices 51-57.

7.3 Look at the index of churches in these CH catalogues for the name of the likely congregation or name of the town and its congregation. This index will provide you with the reference number of the congregation's records, eg Milnathort Antiburgher church is CH3/542. The CH3 records are arranged in numerical order, so look in the CH3 catalogue under the relevant number. Within the list of records of that congregation, you will be looking for records of baptisms or marriages or burials, either as separate volumes or in the same volumes as kirk session minutes: eg Lethendy Associate Congregation Session minute book (CH3/214/1) includes baptisms, 1803-1840. The catalogue will say if there is such a record: normally, minutes do not include such information. Remember that many Free Church congregations did not exist until 1843, when the Free Church was formed by the Disruption from the established Church of Scotland.

7.4 When you are ordering out a volume of these Church records, make sure that your order slip has three numbers, eg CH3/214/1, the second number being the number of the congregation and the third the volume number.

7.5 Some of these church records have been transferred to local archives but the NAS has retained microfilms of many of those records before 1860, which may be consulted. If this is the case it will be noted in the relevant catalogue.

7.6 If the records of the congregation you want are not in the NAS, look in the index to the surveys produced by the National Register of Archives for Scotland (NRAS). Failing that, you should contact the headquarters of that particular church. The addresses of some will be found in The *Church of Scotland Year-Book*.

7.7 *If your ancestor was Roman Catholic,* go to the catalogue labelled RH21. Listed there are photocopies of the surviving records kept by Roman Catholic parish priests of baptisms, marriages and deaths. These are arranged by diocese, but there is an alphabetical list of the parishes at the start of the catalogue, giving the reference number of each. The earliest date is 1703, but most registers do not start until the nineteenth century. There is also a microfilm of the baptismal register of the Catholic Apostolic Church, Edinburgh, 1833-1949 (RH4/174).

7.8 We have to emphasise the incompleteness of all these church records, their existence having depended on the dedication of the clergymen and accident of survival. They are also inconsistent in the details supplied.

7.9 Records of baptisms will usually give the names of the child and of the father, sometimes that of the mother, and in the case of the Roman Catholic records, sometimes those of the god-parents, who may be relatives. If the clergyman chooses, there may occasionally be additional information, eg '4th Sept Margaret Riccalton Dickson daughter of Walter Dickson (above 70 years of age) and his wife Eve Riccalton' (1833 – CH3/667/1).

7.10 Records of marriages will generally give only the name of the marrying couple, but some RC registers invaluably give the parishes in Ireland from where the couple came.

7.11 There are very few death records among the CH3 records and these usually only give the name of the deceased, sometimes the age. Because the Roman Catholic priest needed to give the last sacrament to a dying person, the RC records of deaths are fuller, usually giving the name, age, marital status and cause of death, eg 'John Carley, a married man, was suddenly suffocated in an old coal pit at Campsie by Damp Air' (1815 June 27th – RH21/62/10, p.251).

7.12 There are further records which provide evidence of the birth, marriage and decease of individuals.

Fornication

7.13 The records of both the Church of Scotland and the free churches report the appearance before the kirk session of couples whose extramarital fornication had resulted in the birth of a child. How to gain access to the records of the free churches is already described (7.3). Access to the records of the kirk sessions of the Church of Scotland (CH2) is similar. Go to the volume of the CH2 catalogue, which contains an index of the parishes etc listed in the catalogue. Each parish has a reference number. Look up the volumes listed under that number: each volume has its own number. Order the relevant volume of the kirk session minutes by its reference number, eg CH2/842/2. Such misbehaviour by unmarried couples (whether or not a child was the result) seems to have been the main concern of many kirk sessions before 1900 and their minute books may contain little else. The name of the child will not be given but you will find proof of the birth of a child to a named mother and, with luck, father and the approximate date of birth. An occasional problem arises when the name of the father given by the mother appears to be false. Such entries sometimes demonstrate that the unmarried mother had recently arrived from another parish.

7.14 Cases involving fornication or adultery could be brought by the church before the civil courts. The High Court of Justiciary (see chapter 14) may record such cases until the early eighteenth century, and the authorities had long memories. In Dumfries in 1709, we discover that James Rig of Cairgen was indicted for adultery, 'committed by him about thirty years ago' (JC12/1, p.73). Further evidence of illegitimate births may be found in actions before a sheriff court to order the father to contribute to the maintenance of the child. The record of these actions for aliment will usually provide the names of the mother and father and the date of birth and sex, but not the name, of the child. See 13.36–41 for further explanation of these sheriff court records, which are largely unindexed.

Adoption

7.15 Adoption was not recognised in the law of Scotland until 1930. Adoptions obviously did occur before 1930 but they were informal arrangements and rarely recorded. From 1855, a few may be noted in the Statutory Register of Births when a registrar added that information to the record of birth of a child. The General Register Office for Scotland (see Chapter 4) maintains an Adopted Children Register, which is open to public inspection, as is the original birth entry of an adopted person. However, by law the information connecting the two entries cannot be seen, except by court order, by anyone other than an adopted person who has reached the age of 17 and to whom the information relates, or a local authority or approved adoption agency which is providing counselling. NAS holds records of adoption in the Court of Session records (CS312) and Sheriff Court records, but information may only be supplied from these records to the adopted child having reached the age of 17 or by order of the Court of Session or the Sheriff Court concerned.

Hugh Anderson modr. (101)

1711) May 6th. 711.

The Coll: for ÿ Poor was ── 1·· 3·· 6

May 13th

William Winster (red haird) who long since broke
the acts anent ÿ ware; did this day make his pub:
:tick profession of repentance for ÿ scandal, and pro:
:mising in all time coming to walk orderly was ab:
:solved from the same.   **Winster Warer absol:**

The Coll: for ÿ Poor was ── 1·· 6·· 6

May 20th.

Mr Alexander Anderson Minr att Duffus preach:
:ed in the fore·noon, & our Minr in the afternoon.
After Sermon, the Minr told the people, ÿ our
last School Master, had some time agoe demitted his
office, & now had left ÿ place; & that we endeavour:
:ed, with consent of Sr Robert Gordon; timeously
to provide one fit for ÿ post; that so there might be
no vacancy: and ÿ now he was come and entred nt
the School: and that they might send their children
to him, and give him all suiteable encouragement,
and ÿ it was much their own advantage to do so.
This day Samuel Paply School-mr did precent.   **paply school-mr**

The Coll: for ÿ Poor was ── 1·· 87·· 10.

May 27th.

No Sermon; our minister preaching at Alvis, by
the Presbitries appointment.

June 3d.

The Seamen were publickly admonished, to attend
better in ÿ Afternoon; or that else some oyr course
would be taken to obledge them thereto.   **Sea-men admonishd.**
This day the Session did meet; & after Prayer,
acted as follows:

The Coll: for ÿ Poor was ── 1·· 11·· 4

Alexander Falconer in Cowsea complained upon
Margaret Robertson & Janet Marshal there, for cur:
:sing him: we enjoyned him the next day to give in
his Bill of complaint (with 40 sh.) and told him, we
should yn examine ÿ matter; appointing ÿ Officer
to cite to ÿ diet what wittnesses he pleased.   **Ro'son & marishal cited.**
Also William Hesbin, Elder; complained of Wm
Innes in Stotfold; for frequent cursing and striking
his wife: they, wt what wittnesses ÿ Sr William should
name, were appointed to be summoned to our next
diet.   **& Innes for cursing**
Also complaint was given in against John
Cloggie & Isabel Kintre, both in Kinneddar; that
they were suspected guilty of fornicat'n; they are
appointed to be summoned to our next diet.   **cloggie & Kintre.**
The Minr represented to ÿ Elders; that,
Samuel

Samuel Paply Sess. clk.

*Fornication: the entry at the foot of the page summons to the Kirk
Session a couple accused of fornication (CH2/384/2).*

Legitimation

7.16 The disciplinary procedures of the kirk sessions show that many children were born illegitimate. Some were legitimated by the subsequent marriage of the parents. Others might be legitimated by the Crown or as a consequence of a court declaration.

7.17 Legitimations by the Crown are contained, along with other business, in the records of the Privy Seal (PS). A catalogue of these records has been published for the years 1488-1584 in eight volumes, *The Register of the Privy Seal of Scotland*. Each of these volumes has an index of persons, which will lead you to an entry in the catalogue. At the end of the entry, there is a roman numeral and an arabic numeral, representing respectively the volume and folio number of the original entry in the Privy Seal record. To see the original, which will be in Latin, you order by the reference number PS1 and the volume number, converting it into an arabic numeral (eg PS1/11). For the period between 1585 and 1660, there is no index and you have to use the Privy Seal minute books (PS6/3 and 4), which are written in chronological order. These give only the surname of the person concerned (and what he has been granted, such as legitimation) but provide the volume and folio number in the register (PS1). For the period since 1660, look at the 2-volume index to the Privy Seal 'English record' (ie written in English) held in the NAS. The first volume, up to 1782, indexes persons without distinguishing legitimations, but the second volume does specify them. If you wish to see the original entry in the Privy Seal register, order by PS3 and the volume number. Remember that legitimations might be granted at any age.

Legal records on Marriage and Divorce

7.18 Legitimation can be proved in court by proving the marriage of the parents. Irregular marriages could be recognised by a court of law. Divorce has been possible in Scotland since 1560. From the Reformation until 1830, the court which was responsible for cases involving legitimation and the constitution and dissolution of marriage was the Commissary Court of Edinburgh (CC8). From 1830 until 1984, the responsible court was the Court of Session, though between 1831 and 1835 some cases were still dealt with by the Commissary Court. The Court of Session has adopted a simplified divorce procedure from 1983, which forms a separate series (see 11.19-20). However, since 1984 almost all divorces have been heard by the sheriff courts, and the outcome is recorded by the General Register office for Scotland in the Register of Divorces (see Chapter 4).

7.19 A catalogue of divorce and other consistorial cases heard by the Commissary Court (CC) from 1658 and 1835 is available. This supersedes the calendar of cases published by the Scottish Record Society in 1909, *The Commissariot of Edinburgh – Consistorial Processes and Decreets, 1658-1800* which has an index of persons. The cases cover all aspects of marriage, separation, divorce and legitimacy. In this catalogue, where the description of the case is followed by a roman, then an arabic, numeral, the roman numeral is that of a volume of decrees, which may be ordered by CC8/5 plus the roman numeral (converted into arabic). The arabic numeral is that of the folio on which the report of the case starts. Unless the description includes the words 'no warrants', then the papers in the case will be among the consistorial processes and may be ordered by the reference number CC8/6 and the number of whatever box contains the processes for the relevant date: these numbers may be obtained from the catalogue of Commissary Court records (CC).

7.20 In this catalogue, the description of the case provides the reference of the relevant volume of decrees (CC8/5). Unless the description includes the words 'no warrant', then the papers in the case will be found among the consistorial processes (CC8/6).

7.21 For lawsuits regarding marriage, divorce and legitimacy heard by the Court of Session since 1810, you must go to the records of that Court (see 13.3-20).

Proclamation of Banns of Marriage

7.22 Before a regular marriage took place, the intention to marry had to be publicised by a proclamation in church. As the parties had to pay a fee, kirk session account and cash books sometimes give the names of couples about to marry, in such terms as 'To cash received from James Kirk in Auchterderran when contracted with Catherine Haxton in this Parish' (Kipglassie, 1783 June 6, CH2/406/7). Unfortunately, many of these account book entries simply state 'Proclamation' and the amount paid, omitting the names of the parties. If you wish to follow this line of inquiry, the relevant records are listed in the CH2 catalogue, described in 7.13.

Marriage Contracts

7.23 Until recently, it was the practice, when members of propertied families got married, for a marriage contract to be drawn up, whereby the families made financial provision for the couple, particularly for the future financial security of the wife and children. These contracts could be drawn up either before or after the marriage ceremony. You would expect to find in a marriage contract the names of the couple and their fathers and possibly other relatives. The date of the contract would usually but not necessarily be close to the date of the marriage. As these were private documents, there is no guarantee that the one you are seeking has survived, but the following groups of records should be consulted.

7.24 Registers of Deeds (RD, SC, etc) – see 12.2-17. One difficulty in searching for marriage contracts in this source is that a marriage contract might be registered years after the date of the marriage, perhaps after the death of the husband. There was no compulsion to register a marriage contract.

7.25 Register of Sasines (RS). As many marriage contracts included provisions for a liferent income from land, the subsequent instrument of sasine should be recorded in a Register of Sasines – see 10.3-18.

7.26 Gifts and Deposits (GD). If either of the parties was a member of a family whose records have been gifted to or deposited in the National Archives of Scotland, then their marriage contract may be among these records – see 6.19-20.

7.27 Miscellaneous papers – Marriage Contracts (RH9/7). This is a collection of 306 miscellaneous marriage contracts. They are arranged and listed in two series, the first chronological from 1591 to 1846 and the second rather haphazardly arranged but dated between 1605 and 1811. They are not indexed but are clearly catalogued in the RH9 catalogue.

7.28 One should bear in mind that occasionally a marriage contract was not followed by a marriage (see 13.57).

Irregular Marriages

7.29 Until 1940, irregular marriages, in the form of a declaration by the parties before witnesses, but not before an established clergyman, were perfectly legal. However, such marriages were frowned upon. The parties might be rebuked by their kirk session and they and their witnesses were liable to be fined. Thus evidence of such marriages may be found in kirk session minutes described in 7.13 and in JP and burgh court records (see 13.48-50). They are further explained in the introduction to *Calendar of Irregular Marriages in the South Leith Kirk Session Records* 1697-1818 (Scottish Record Society). The Ewart Library in Dumfries is the best source of information about irregular marriages at Gretna Green. The NAS has copies of registers of similar marriages at Lamberton Toll, Berwickshire, 1833–1849 (RH2/8/84).

Inhibitions

7.30 Evidence of marriage might also appear when a husband stopped his liability for his wife's debts (see 13.58-60).

Fatal Accidents

7.31 The Fatal Accidents Inquiry (Scotland) Act, 1895, provided for public inquiries by sheriff and jury into fatal accidents occurring in industrial employment or occupations. If you are looking for information about a fatal accident at work, you should look at the catalogue of the records of the relevant sheriff court (see 13.38). The contents list will give you the reference number of the fatal accident inquiry records. There are none earlier than 1895. You should find the name of the widow, employment and employers of the deceased, and the date and cause of death. These records are not indexed and there are gaps in the records for many courts for parts of the twentieth century.

Mortcloth and Burial Records

7.32 It used to be common for the kirk session of the parish church to hire out a mortcloth to cover a dead body during the funeral service. The kirk session accounts, by recording a payment for a mortcloth, give the approximate date of death of the deceased. Records of mortcloth payments may appear in the kirk session minutes or account books (CH2 – see 7.13) or in the accounts kept by the heritors (HR – see 10.41). Such accounts may also include payments for coffins or digging the grave of named persons.

7.33 A few of the CH2 kirk session records include records of burials, specified in the list of records of that kirk session. Among the burgh records in the National Archives of Scotland, there are cemetery records for Dunbar,

1879-1902 (B18/18/24) and Tranent, 1885-1949 (B77/5/2-4). However, cemetery records are mostly held by the District Council in whose area the cemetery lies and enquiries in the first instance should be made to the Chief Executive or Superintendent of Cemeteries of the appropriate district council. The NAS holds very few district council records and the only burial records therein are those of Prestonpans – look up DC2/5/23-28 in the District Council catalogue (DC). Such burial records may be more concerned with the purchaser of a place of burial than with who is actually buried there.

7.34 The records of the Edinburgh Cemetery Company, which administered seven cemeteries in the city and which were formerly held on temporary deposit by the National Archives of Scotland, have now been transferred permanently to Edinburgh City Archives.

7.35 The inscriptions on gravestones are usually of great genealogical value. The microfilm series (RH4) includes copies of monumental inscriptions noted by S Cramer in burial grounds in various parts of Scotland (RH4/16 and 41). Look at Appendix 13 in the RH4 catalogue for the full list of these burial grounds.

7.36 A survey of monumental inscriptions throughout Scotland was begun by the Scottish Genealogy Society some years ago. These are arranged in volumes by county or part-county, in which the arrangement is by alphabetical order of churchyard with an index of surnames for each churchyard. A similar series of monumental inscriptions in North Ayrshire has been compiled by the local council. Copies of all these volumes are in the NAS library. You may also be able to find them in a local library.

Anatomy

7.37 Not all bodies go directly to their grave. Some are supplied to schools of anatomy for the benefit of the students. Since 1842, the Inspector of Anatomy for Scotland has kept registers that are preserved in the NAS as part of the records of the Ministry of Health. Look at the MH catalogue where these registers are listed under the reference MH1. There were schools of anatomy at Aberdeen, Dundee, Edinburgh, Glasgow and St Andrews. There is a 50-year closure period on this record. The registers are arranged chronologically and give the name, age, sex, last place of abode (typically the Royal Infirmary or Charity Workhouse), and date, place and cause of death, of each deceased. The registers are not indexed.

∞ 8 ∞

Inheritance: Wills and Executries

8.1 Apart from the records of births, marriages and deaths, the most useful records for genealogical research are those which deal with inheritance and the disposal of the property of a deceased person. Searching for wills and testaments and related records up to 1901 has been transformed by the Scottish Documents digitisation project, part of the Scottish Archive Network (*www.scottishdocuments.com*). This resource provides access to images of the principal testamentary records held in the NAS, and its indexes have superseded all the existing finding aids, both published and unpublished. The following sections therefore offer a supplementary guide to searching the testamentary records for the period to 1901, and more detailed guidance for the period since 1902.

8.2 In legal terms, property may be either heritable or moveable, and, until 1964, the rules of inheritance in Scotland were different in respect of heritable and moveable property. Heritable property is basically land, minerals in the ground, and buildings. Moveable property is basically property that can be moved, such as money, furniture, animals, machinery and implements. Because of this distinction, the information about inheritance in heritable and moveable property is kept in different records and therefore is best considered separately. In this chapter, we shall consider the records that concern the disposal of moveable property of a person who has died.

8.3 When a person dies, an executor should be appointed to administer the moveable estate of the deceased. If the deceased has left a will, then the executor will usually be appointed by the will, though this appointment will require confirmation by the relevant court. If the deceased has died intestate (i.e. has not left a will), then the executor will be appointed and confirmed by the court. Thus the records which concern us are the records of the confirmation of executors, whether or not there is a will. These records are known as testaments, a testament–testamentar if there is a will,

Volume containing the testament and inventory of Niel Gow, 1808 (CC7/6/7).

a testament-dative if there is none. Each testament will give the name and designation of the deceased, usually the date of death, the confirmation of the executor, an inventory of the moveable estate of the deceased (which may include household furniture, implements of trade, and debts owed to and by the deceased), and the will, if there is one.

8.4 The relevant court was a commissary court (CC) until the 1820s and thereafter a sheriff court (SC). Obviously, before you search for the will or executry of an ancestor, it helps to know the approximate year of death and where in Scotland he or she lived.

8.5 Before investigating the relevant records, you should be aware of certain snags.

a. Not only did very few people leave wills, but, in the majority of cases, the family of a deceased person did not bother with the formality of confirming an executry. 'We keepit siller in the crap o' the wa', jist stappit in. We had nae lawyers, a' body just fechted it oot amang themselves.' *(Innes Review,* vol. VII, no.11).

b. Some records have not survived because of the depredations of fire and other accidents.

c. As an eldest son inherited the whole of the heritable property of his deceased father, he did not receive any of the moveable property in intestacy and therefore the eldest son's name may be omitted from his father's testament.

d. If the deceased had died in debt, his nearest of kin might not wish to take on his executry (and therefore liability to his creditors). Thus sometimes a creditor is named as executor. In such a case, the testament is unlikely to contain genealogical information.

e. Testaments are usually confirmed within a year of death, but this is not always so, eg Captain James Carmichael died at Nairn on 17 May 1813 but his executry was not confirmed until 30 October 1827 (SC26/39/1, p. 326).

Executries before 1824

8.6 If your ancestor died before 1824, then the relevant court is a commissary court. There are records for 22 such courts covering different parts of Scotland. The commissary courts acquired the jurisdiction of the pre-Reformation church courts and the areas they administered (known as commissariots) were based on the areas of these church courts, which are different from any modern administrative areas.

8.7   Thanks to Scottish Documents it is unnecessary to discover which commissary court or courts cover the area in which your ancestor lived in order to find a will. However, it can be useful to do so for exploring other commissary court records (see 7.18-20). A useful series of maps published by the Institute of Heraldic and Genealogical Studies, Northgate, Canterbury, Kent, gives the boundaries of the commissariots and the parishes which lay within them: a set of these maps is kept in the Historical Search Room. Other guides to which parishes were in which commissariots are mentioned in 2.4. However, changes in parish boundaries and the irregularity of the bounds of the commissariots mean that it may be easier for you to use the following table which simply shows modern counties and their equivalent commissariots. It is worth remembering that you may find an executry in the commissary court of Edinburgh rather than the local commissary court because, while Edinburgh dealt mainly with the executries of people who lived within the commissariot of Edinburgh, it could also confirm the executors of people who lived elsewhere and particularly those who died furth of Scotland.

County	*Commissariot*	*Reference Numbers*
Aberdeen	Aberdeen	CC1
	Moray	CC16
Angus (Forfar)	Brechin	CC3
	Dunkeld	CC7
	St Andrews	CC20
Argyll	Argyll	CC2
	The Isles	CC12
Ayr	Glasgow	CC9
Banff	Aberdeen	CC1
	Moray	CC16
Berwick	Lauder	CC15
Bute	The Isles	CC12
Caithness	Caithness	CC4
Clackmannan	Dunblane	CC6
	Stirling	CC21
Dumfries	Dumfries	CC5
Dunbarton	Glasgow	CC9
	Hamilton and Campsie	CC10

County	Commissariot	Reference Numbers
East Lothian		
(Haddington)	Edinburgh	CC8
	Dunkeld	CC7
Edinburgh City	Edinburgh	CC8
Fife	Dunkeld	CC7
	St Andrews	CC20
	Stirling	CC21
Glasgow City	Glasgow	CC9
	Hamilton and Campsie	CC10
Inverness	Argyll	CC11
	Inverness	CC11
	The Isles	CC12
Kincardine	Brechin	CC3
	St Andrews	CC20
Kinross	St Andrews	CC20
	Stirling	CC21
Kirkcudbright	Dumfries	CC5
	Kirkcudbright	CC13
	Wigtown	CC22
Lanark	Glasgow	CC9
	Hamilton and Campsie	CC10
	Lanark	CC14
Midlothian (Edinburgh)	Edinburgh	CC8
Moray (Elgin)	Moray	CC16
Nairn	Moray	CC16
Orkney	Orkney and Shetland	CC17
Peebles	Peebles	CC18
Perth	Dunblane	CC6
	Dunkeld	CC7
	St Andrews	CC20
Renfrew	Glasgow	CC9
	Hamilton and Campsie	CC10
Ross and Cromarty	The Isles	CC12
	Ross	CC19
Roxburgh	Peebles	CC18
Selkirk	Peebles	CC18
Shetland	Orkney and Shetland	CC17
Stirling	Glasgow	CC9
	Hamilton and Campsie	CC10

County	Commissariot	Reference Numbers
	Stirling	CC21
Sutherland	Caithness	CC4
West Lothian		
(Linlithgow)	Edinburgh	CC8
	Dunkeld	CC7
Wigtown	Wigtown	CC22

8.8 The printed indexes to the 'Commissariot Records', published by the Scottish Record Society (1897-1904) have been completely superseded by the search facilities of Scottish Documents. For the period 1801-1824 the old typescript indexes have also been superseded by Scottish Documents. However, some of the same principles apply to searching the information. Married women are indexed under their maiden name, but can also be searched for under their married name. Other forms of electronic searching include searching by surname, forename, occupations or designation, date, commissary or sheriff court, and places. Variant spellings can be used, and there are many other useful search tools to help you get the most from the index.

8.9 The original registers of testaments are no longer available for general consultation, and you should either use Scottish Documents or consult the electronic versions of the registers in the NAS.

8.10 In the NAS search rooms, having found the person you are looking for in the index, you will be able to consult the electronic image of the testament you want. Alternatively you can browse the contents of the registers electronically. As most volumes are arranged chronologically by dates of confirmation, it should not be too difficult to choose the correct part of the volume. The name of the deceased is usually placed clearly in the margin, sometimes with the date of confirmation, or the date of confirmation should appear in the last or second last paragraph of the testament. There is often no gap between one testament and the next, so look for the words 'The Testament' ('Dative' or 'Testamentar') which starts each testament. The testaments usually provide the name of the spouse and children, and other relations who were beneficiaries or executors.

8.11 Sometimes, a volume of a register of testaments has not survived but related documents called 'warrants' (see 6.16) have done so. Many of the warrants which act as a substitute for a lost register have been digitally imaged for Scottish Documents. The following commissariots have been covered in this way: Aberdeen, Brechin, Kirkcudbright, St Andrews, Stirling and Wigtown. For other commissary courts the warrants have not been digitally imaged. The printed indexes should indicate warrants with a letter 'T' or 'W', and they can also be identified in the indexes in Scottish Documents. Consult the CC catalogue for the reference number of the warrants of testaments which are arranged by box or bundle.

8.12 The Register of Testaments and most other records of Aberdeen Commissary Court were destroyed by fire in 1722. Afterwards, copies of some earlier testaments and other writs were collected into a series now referenced CC1/15. These are not indexed but are listed in a minute book (CC1/11/9). The testaments date back into the seventeenth century.

8.13 Where a series of testaments or warrants is lacking, other papers in the commissary records, for example edicts, may provide details such as the names of executors. For example, supplementary documents in the Argyll commissary court records (CC2) have been described in detail in a catalogue of records which complement the register of testaments: *Argyll Commissary Court: A Calendar of testaments, inventories, commissary processes and other records, 1700-1825.* This was compiled by Mr W Bigwood, Flat B, The Lodge, 2 East Road, North Berwick, EH39 4HN, from whom copies may be purchased; the index may also be consulted in the Historical Search Room.

Executries between the 1820s and 1875

8.14 By the Commissary Courts (Scotland) Act, 1823, the commissary courts ceased to exist on 1 January 1824 and their jurisdiction in executry matters was transferred to the sheriff courts, which now became responsible for confirming executors. An important exception to the transition was that Edinburgh, Haddington and Linlithgow remained part of the commissariot of Edinburgh until 1830. Elsewhere the transfer was not made precisely and there is considerable overlap between the testamentary records of the commissary courts and those of the sheriff courts, both before and after January 1824. The Scottish Documents project has imaged the overlapping records, so that in these cases the reader can choose between different versions of the same testamentary records. Generally the version taking up more pages (indicated in the index) will be clearer because the writing will be less cramped. The following table of counties shows the end dates of the commissary court records and the start dates of the sheriff court records.

County	Commissariot	Sheriff Court
Aberdeen	1823	1824 (SC1)
Angus (Forfar)	1823	1824 (SC47)
Argyll	1823	1815 (SC51)
Ayr	1823	1824 (SC6)
Banff	1827	1824 (SC2)
Berwick	1823	1823 (SC60)
Bute	1823	1824 (SC8)
Caithness	1827	1824 (SC14)
Clackmannan	1825	1824 (SC64)
Dumfries	1823	1827 (SC15)
Dunbarton	1823	1824 (SC65)
East Lothian (Haddington)	1829	1808 (SC70)
Edinburgh City	1829	1808 (SC70)
Fife	1823	1824 (SC20)
Glasgow	1823	1824 (SC36)
Inverness	1824	1825 (SC29)
Kincardine	1823	1824 (SC5)
Kinross	1825	1824 (SC64)
Kirkcudbright	1824	1824 (SC16)
Lanark	1823	1824 (SC36)
Midlothian (Edinburgh)	1829	1808 (SC70)
Moray (Elgin)	1827	1824 (SC26)
Nairn	1827	1824 (SC26)
Orkney	1832	1824 (SC11)
Peebles	1827	1814 (SC42)
Perth	1825	1824 (SC44 & 49)
Renfrew	1823	1824 (SC58)
Ross and Cromarty	1824	1824 (SC25 & 33)
Roxburgh	1827	1827 (SC62)
Selkirk	1827	1824 (SC63)
Shetland	1826	1827 (SC12)
Stirling	1823	1809 (SC67)
Sutherland	1827	1799 (SC9)
West Lothian (Linlithgow)	1829	1808 (SC70)
Wigtown	1826	1826 (SC19)

8.15 Each sheriff court had its own way of organising its executry (or commissary) records, so the records are not arranged consistently. Sometimes there are three separate series of commissary records, all of which you may wish to examine, but sometimes two or all three series may be combined. Though the names they were given also vary (eg 'commissary record books'), the basic three are records of confirmations (of executries), wills ('settlements', 'testamentary deeds'), and inventories (of the moveable estate of the deceased). Remember that if your ancestor died intestate, then there will be no will, although there may be an inventory of moveable estate.

8.16 Wills were normally recorded in the sheriff court for the county in which the person lived. When a person lived outwith Scotland, but died leaving moveable property within Scotland, then confirmation of the executry was the responsibility of the commissary office of the sheriff court of Edinburgh (SC70). The following table shows each modern county and the equivalent sheriff court which dealt with commissary business between the 1820s and 1875.

County	Sheriff Court	Reference Number
Aberdeen	Aberdeen	SC1
Angus (Forfar)	Dundee (from 1832)	SC45
	Forfar	SC47
Argyll	Dunoon	SC51
Ayr	Ayr	SC6
Banff	Banff	SC2
Berwick	Duns	SC60
Bute	Rothesay	SC8
Caithness	Wick	SC14
Clackmannan	Alloa	SC64
Dumfries	Dumfries	SC15
Dunbarton	Dumbarton	SC65
East Lothian (Haddington)	Haddington (from 1830)	SC40
Edinburgh City	Edinburgh	SC70
Fife	Cupar	SC20
Glasgow City	Glasgow	SC36
Inverness	Inverness	SC29
Kincardine	Stonehaven	SC5
Kinross	Alloa (to 1847)	SC64
	Kinross (from 1847)	SC22
Kirkcudbright	Kirkcudbright	SC16
Lanark	Glasgow	SC36

County	Sheriff Court	Reference Number
Midlothian (Edinburgh)	Edinburgh	SC70
Moray (Elgin)	Elgin	SC26
Nairn	Elgin (to 1838)	SC26
	Nairn (from 1839)	SC31
Orkney	Kirkwall	[In Kirkwall]
Peebles	Peebles	SC42
Perth	Dunblane	SC44
	Perth	SC49
Renfrew	Paisley	SC58
Ross	Dingwall	SC25
	Stornoway (to 1850)	SC33
Roxburgh	Jedburgh	SC62
Selkirk	Selkirk	SC63
Shetland	Lerwick	[In Lerwick]
Stirling	Stirling	SC67
Sutherland	Dornoch	SC9
West Lothian (Linlithgow)	Linlithgow (from 1830)	SC41
Wigtown	Wigtown	SC19

8.17 If your ancestor lived within the jurisdiction of any other sheriff court in Scotland and died between 1846 and 1867, or in the case of Edinburgh, Haddington and Linlithgow, between 1827 and 1865, you may wish to look at a series of printed indexes entitled *Index to Personal Estates of Defuncts*. Although they have been almost entirely superseded by Scottish Documents, the entries do contain two useful details which are not found in the Scottish Documents index: the date of death, noted at the end of each entry, and a code letter telling you whether the person died testate or intestate. Each volume contains a group of counties, within which the deceased are indexed in alphabetical order. Within each surname, the men are listed before the women.

8.18 In many instances the inventory states that a will was registered in the 'Sheriff Court Books' of the county. These sheriff court books are the Register of Deeds of the particular sheriff court (see further in 12.13) and you should find another copy of the will recorded in a volume of the Register of Deeds.

8.19 If your ancestor lived furth of Scotland, but owned property in Scotland, then the sheriff court of Edinburgh (SC70) was responsible for his executry.

If his executry was confirmed before 1858 or you simply want to see the inventory of his Scottish property, then you search as if he had died in Edinburgh. If the executry was confirmed between 1858 and 1900 and he lived in England or Ireland, there will be a copy of the English or Irish probate in the Probates Resealed series (SC70/6). The whole series up to 1900 has been included in the Scottish Documents digitising project and is available on the same basis as the digitised registers of testaments.

Executries from 1876 to 1901

8.20 For the period from 1876 to 1901 the wills have been digitally imaged and fully indexed by Scottish Documents. The index provides the full references of the records, and it has largely superseded the annual printed volumes of the *Calendar of Confirmations*.

Each index entry gives the name and designation of the deceased, the date and place of death, whether testate or intestate, and where and when confirmation was granted.

A typical entry reads:

> 13 November 1891
> STEVENSON, James
> Mason, residing at New Cross, Beith, who died 24 July 1891,
> at Beith, testate

8.21 The details which you can find in the *Calendar* which have been excluded from the Scottish Documents index are the dates when the will was made and recorded, the name of the executor and the value of the estate. The Historical Search Room holds a full set from 1875 to 1901. Several of the larger Scottish libraries and some archives also hold copies of the *Calendar*.

Executries from 1902

8.22 From 1902 to 1959, there is a series of annual printed volumes called the *Calendar of Confirmations and Inventories*, as noted above. The Historical Search Room has a set; thereafter the series may be consulted on microfiche in the Legal Search Room. Several of the larger Scottish libraries and some archives also hold copies of the printed *Calendar*.

8.23 This *Calendar* indexes all those persons whose executry has been confirmed in Scotland in that particular year, regardless of where they lived.

The index is in strict alphabetical order, except that some entries may appear in addenda at the end of the volume. Married women are indexed only under their married name. If you do not find the entry you want in the year of death, check the subsequent years.

8.24 Each entry gives the name and designation of the deceased, the date and place of death, whether testate or intestate, where and when confirmation was granted, the name and designation of the executor and the value of the estate. If the deceased was testate, you are given the date of the will and the court books in which it has been recorded and when. Additional inventories ('eiks') are usually noted by hand. To investigate further, note the name of the sheriff court where confirmation was granted (which is in heavier type), the date of confirmation, and, if there is a will, in which court and when it was recorded.

8.25 For example, if you look up 'HARDIE, James Keir, M.P.' in the *Calendar of Confirmations and Inventories* for 1915, you find that confirmation to his wife and daughter as executors was granted at AYR on 28 December and that his will was recorded in the court books of the commissariot of Ayr on 27 December. You therefore look at the Ayr Sheriff Court catalogue (SC6). You find that the confirmation of his executors is in the volume referenced SC61/48/56, but you are more likely to want to see his inventory and will. The Register of Inventories is SC6/44 and the volume which covers December 1915 is SC6/44/77, while the Register of Testamentary Writings is SC6/46 and the volume including December 1915 is SC6/46/42. Both of these are arranged chronologically and you will find the inventory and will each recorded under the date 27 December 1915, i.e. they had to be recorded before confirmation was granted the next day, 28 December.

8.26 From 1960 until 1984 the Calendar of Confirmations took the form of index cards for each year, which are only available on microfiche in the Legal Search Room. Each index card contains the name of the deceased, whether they were testate or intestate, the sheriff court, and the date of confirmation of the executors. Using the date provided you then need to consult the relevant sheriff court catalogue as above to identify the reference(s) of the volume(s) covering the confirmation date. If the confirmations are in a separate series, you will first need to order out the confirmation in order to establish the date on which the testament and inventory and any eiks (additional inventories) were recorded, usually several days or weeks earlier.

8.27 After 1985 testaments, inventories and confirmations from all the sheriff courts were microfilmed by the Commissary Office in Edinburgh. A copy of the microfilm (SC70/17) and the electronic index are available in NAS after 10 years. Enquiries for testamentary records up to 10 years old should be directed to the Sheriff Clerk's Office, Commissary Section, Sheriff Court House, 27 Chambers Street, Edinburgh EH1 1LB (Tel. 0131 225 2525, Fax 0131 225 4422, E-mail: *cru@scotcourts.gov*.

8.28 For wills of persons dying furth of Scotland after 1901, you need to consult the typed index to the Probates Resealed in the Historical Search Room, which gives you a date. Alternatively you can find the entries in the *Calendar of Confirmations*. You must then look up SC70/6 in the catalogue to find the reference number which includes that date. These probates do not include the inventory of goods belonging to the deceased in Scotland. That information is in the Edinburgh Register of Inventories (SC70/1).

Wills Elsewhere

8.29 If you have been unable to find a record of your ancestor's executry in the Commissary Court and Sheriff Court commissary records, there are other sources you can try.

8.30 RH9/8 is a collection of miscellaneous executry papers, 1481-1882. The catalogue is based on the index published by the Scottish Record Society in 1904.

8.31 If your ancestor was a member of a family whose records have been gifted to or deposited in the NAS, then a copy of a testament may survive among the records of that GD (see 6.19).

8.32 Mention has been made above of wills recorded in the 'Sheriff Court Books'. Many wills are registered in various other registers of deeds, which are described in Chapter 10. As explained there, not all of these are indexed and therefore easy to search. What is loosely termed as a 'will' may appear under different names, 'Latter Will and Testament', 'Deed of Settlement', 'Trust Disposition and Settlement', 'Mutual Disposition and Settlement', etc. Dispositions and settlements were often used to get round the rule that heritable property could not be bequeathed. Wills thus registered are likely to be those of better-off folk and of course none should be registered till after the death of the testator.

8.33 Separate series of wills of servicemen exist for the twentieth century, mainly for the First and Second World Wars (SC70/8-10). See Chapter 17 for further details.

8.34 Printed calendars of *Probate and Letters of Administration* for England and Wales were provided for the use of the Commissary Office in Edinburgh. This set, covering the years 1858-1970, may be consulted in the Historical Search Room (SC70/13).

8.35 NAS occasionally receives claims by people seeking to trace money supposedly left by ancestors who died intestate, and whose money has allegedly been 'left in Chancery'. These bequests are almost invariably mythical. In rare cases where the beneficiary of a will could not be traced, the property concerned had to be reported to the Queen's (or King's) Lord Treasurer's Remembrancer. In cases of an intestate person with no known heirs, their property fell to the Crown as *ultimus haeres* (the last heir). See 9.31-38 for further information.

Death Duties

8.36 Connected with the records of executries are estate duty records (IRS5-4). These may not give any genealogical information other than what you can obtain from the commissary and sheriff court records, which you should investigate first.

8.37 The estate duty records are part of the records of the Inland Revenue in Scotland and begin in 1804. Look first at the detailed explanation on 'Estate Duty Office Registers' contained in the IRS catalogue. There are various series of books and registers, relating to the various taxes which have been levied on the estates of deceased persons. There is a 75-year closure on these records. The categories of estate duty register and the useful non-financial information you might find in them are as follows. The indexes usually give only the relevant folio, and the relevant volume has to be discovered from a study of the IRS catalogue.

- **IRS5** Personal Legacy Registers, 1804-1829. These state the relationship of the legatees to the deceased, though not always very specifically, eg 'Mrs Amelia Farquharson, descend' of Brother of mother' (IRS5/3).
- **IRS6** Return Ledgers for Inventory Duty, 1831-1892, which account for repayments when there has been over-payments. Date of death. May give name of lawyer.

- **IRS7** Residue Duty Account Books, 1819-1838, account for payments of inventory duty. Name of executor. Indexes, 1808-1850 and 1885-1897, which are indexes to the inventories which are numbered.

- **IRS8** Legacy Receipt Books, 1796-1865. Relationship of legatees.

- **IRS9** Register of Inventories received from Commissary offices, 1824-1876. Indexes, 1863-1884.

- **IRS10** Testate Register and Indexes, 1828-1879. Date of death. Executor. Relationship of legatees.

- **IRS11** Intestate Register and Indexes, 1829-1879. Executor. Persons beneficially entitled and their relationship. Solicitors.

- **IRS12** Succession Duty Register and Indexes, 1853-1868. Date of death. This record relates to succession in heritable subjects (i.e. land and houses mainly) which could not be transferred by an ordinary will until 1868. The entries explain why the named successor is succeeding to the heritable property, whether by a legal document or in right of a relationship.

- **IRS13** General Registers, 1880-1906. Date of death. Relationship of beneficiaries.

- **IRS14** Indexes, 1870-1907, to IRS10, 11, 12 and 13. Date of death. Closed for only 30 years.

❧ *9* ❧

Inheriting Houses and Land in Scotland

9.1   This chapter is concerned with the records of inheritance of heritable property (houses and land). Clearly, this will matter to you only if your ancestor was likely to have owned his own house or land. Most Scots did not.

9.2   Historically, the system of land-holding in Scotland was a feudal one. In theory, land belonged to the Crown, but the Crown granted land to subjects, who could then make grants to others, while retaining certain rights. Before 1868, heirs had to prove their entitlement as heritable property could not be bequeathed. The need of an heir to prove his right to inherit created records which are useful to the genealogist. However, the death of a landowner did not inevitably or immediately result in such a record. Often, the heir simply occupied the lands and did not go through the correct procedures for years. A landowner might grant lands to his eldest son, reserving rights to himself during his lifetime. After 1868, heritable property could be bequeathed. However an heir acquired a property, any such transfer of ownership should after 1617 be recorded in the Register of Sasines (see 10.3 onwards).

9.3   Where there had been no grant or bequest by a deceased property owner, until 1964 the law of primogeniture applied. By this the eldest son inherited all the heritable property, excluding his siblings. If there were no sons but there were daughters, all the daughters inherited equally.

Retours (Services of Heirs)

9.4   The most accessible record of the transfer of heritable property is the record of Retours, which are part of the Chancery records (C). When a subject of the Crown died, his heir had to prove his right to inherit his ancestor's lands by the procedure of an inquest and 'retour' (= return) to Chancery. Retours could also be used by less exalted folk to provide evidence of their right to the heritable property of an ancestor. Retours which specified the lands were called special retours. General retours did not name any lands. These special and general retours, which are also known as services of heirs, will tell you the names of the heir and the ancestor, their relationship and sometimes the date of death of the ancestor.

9.5   The retour procedure was also used to appoint a tutor to administer the affairs of a fatherless child (a 'pupil', under 14 if a boy, 12 if a girl). The tutor was usually the nearest adult male relative of the father.

9.6   The retours date from 1530 and are in Latin until 1847 (excepting the years 1652-1659). They are indexed throughout but the style of indexes changes dramatically after 1700. The year 1700 is covered in both series of indexes.

Retours before 1700

9.7   A summary of the retours up to 1700 was published in 2 volumes in 1811 and an index thereto in a third volume in 1816. The 3 volumes are entitled *Inquisitionum ad Capellam Regis Retornatarum Abbreviatio*. The title on the spines of the volumes in the Historical Search Room is shortened to *Inquisitionum Retornatarum Abbreviatio*. The Scottish Genealogy Society has also produced a CD-ROM for the years 1544-1699. The summaries and indexes of the special retours are arranged separately within counties. Look in volume 3 under the county in which your ancestor owned land. Under each county, there is an index of names ('Index Nominum') and an index of places ('Index Locorum'). Also look under the headings 'Inquisitiones Generales' and 'Inquisitiones de Tutela' at the 'Index Nominum' of each. Heir, ancestor, tutor and pupil are all indexed.

9.8   An awkwardness in using these indexes is that names are printed as they appear in the original document, the forenames in their Latin form, and the surnames in variant spellings (eg 'Garden' may appear as 'Gairdin') and therefore not in the form or order you might expect.

9.9   In each index, each name is followed by a number. This number is the running number of the summaries. You then go to volume 1 or 2 and look up that number under the particular county within the 'Inquisitiones Speciales', or under the 'Inquisitiones Generales' or under the 'Inquisitiones de Tutela', depending on the index in which you have found the number. If the entries in a county within the 'Inquisitiones Speciales' seem not to go up to the number you have, then look at the supplementary pages in volume 2 which follow the entries for Wigton.

9.10 Most summaries are in Latin. Each summary is headed by its date, then you get the name of the heir, the name of the ancestor, and the relationship, and, in the 'Inquisitiones Speciales', the lands. The date of death is not given, though it may appear in the original record of special retours. In the 'Inquisitiones de Tutela', the first name is that of the tutor, followed by his relationship to his 'pupil' (the child), whose name follows. At the end of each summary, you will find a roman number (= the volume number) and an arabic number (= the folio number) or you will find a letter of the alphabet followed by an arabic number. If you want to see the full document in the Chancery records, you order by the reference C22 and the volume number, converting that number into an arabic one. The letter references A to I represent volumes now numbered C22/177-185 (look at the C catalogue for the details). Thus, if the reference is G.172, you order out C22/183 and, having obtained that volume, look up folio 172.

9.11 If you have failed to find your ancestor in the *Inquisitionum Retornatarum Abbreviatio*, then look at the very end of the Historical Search Room copy of volume 11, where you will find four inserted pages, printed in 1900, containing abridgements, in the same format but arranged alphabetically by name of heir, of a few retours from 1303 to 1622 omitted from the official register, but rescued by a Mr Alexander Macdonald. To read the full text of these retours, you order out C39/4 (a volume of transcripts). The number at the end of each abridgement is the folio number in that volume.

9.12 As there was no time limit for recording retours, some pre-1700 retours were recorded after 1700, occasionally well after.

Retours from 1700

9.13 Starting in 1700 and up to the present day, there is a series of printed 'Indexes to the Services of Heirs in Scotland', decennial up to 1859, annual thereafter, with the title 'Services of Heirs' on the spine. There is more than one decennial or annual index in each volume. These are indexes to the general and special retours, but they do not index the appointments of tutors. Before using these indexes for the first time, you should read the 'explanations' which introduce the volume for 1700–1749.

9.14 These indexes index by name of the heir ('the Person Served') not the ancestor, but at the end of each volume or ten-year period there is a supplement, which lists alphabetically the names of ancestors ('Persons Served to') whose heirs do not have the same surname, cross-referring to the names of the heirs. In the index, after the name of the heir, you will find 'distinguishing particulars', i.e. the heir's designation, the relationship and name of the ancestor, sometimes the latter's date of death, what type of heir, the lands if he is heir special, and the date of the retour. There follows the date of recording and a monthly number: note both of these if you are to proceed further.

9.15 To obtain the call number of the service of heir itself, you must look in the C catalogue under C22 up to 15 November 1847 and after that date under C28. Choose the volume which includes the date of recording you have found in the index. In that volume, look for the date of recording and the monthly running number, both of which will appear in the margin of the text.

9.16 For example, say you are interested in James Duncan, son of John Duncan, minister in Zetland [Shetland], who in 1736 was served heir to his uncle Henry Robertson, apothecary in Edinburgh. The index tells you that the date of recording was 1736 November 24 and the monthly number is 14. The volume for that date is C22/64. The entries in the volume are in chronological order and you read in the margin 'no 14 of novr. 1736' beside the copy of the retour, which explains in detail the relationship between the deceased and his heir.

9.17 The date of death of the ancestor is sometimes stated, but more often is not. In the simpler entries of sons succeeding fathers, there may be no additional information in the text (in Latin until 1847) than there is in the index (in English).

9.18 If you are looking for a service of heir between 1700 and 1796 and cannot find it in the 'Services of Heirs' in its proper place, try the one-page 'List of Unrecorded Retours' which is placed in Volume 5 of the 'Services of Heirs' between 1905 and 1906. Those listed which start with the letters A–J will be found by ordering out C25/10 and with letters L–Y in C25/11.

9.19 If you are looking for a service of heir between 1792 and 1846 and cannot find it in the 'Services of Heirs', try the 'Index of Retours of General Service', which were dated before 1847 but recorded after 1859. This index is also placed in Volume 5 of the 'Services of Heirs' between 1905 and 1906. You will find these retours either in C22/175 or 176, depending on the date of recording.

9.20 If you are looking for the retour of the appointment of a tutor to administer the affairs of a child, there is a typed index covering the period 1701-1886 (which index also covers the appointment of curators to administer the affairs of insane persons until 1897). The index is by name of the child and gives the volume and folio numbers of the record. Order by the reference C22 and the volume number. There are no such retours after 1886, as this method of administering the affairs of a child had fallen into disuse, having gradually been replaced by an alternative method, that of the appointment of a factor loco tutoris by the Court of Session (see 13.25), or, after 1880, by a sheriff court if the estate was small (see 13.38-45).

Inquests

9.21 The decision that someone was indeed the heir of a deceased person or the right person to be tutor to a fatherless child was made locally by an inquest. The decision of the inquest was then 'retoured' to Chancery. At the beginning of every retour, we are told in which sheriff or burgh court the inquest was held. Sometimes, but only sometimes, the sheriff court preserved the records of the inquest and these records may provide further family details (and are in English). For example, in the Register of Retours we are told simply that, in 1844, Thomas Crocket, plasterer in Dumfries, was served heir to his great-grandfather, Andrew Thomson, slater in Dumfries (C22/166). The equivalent sheriff court records provide the names of Thomas's parents, grandparents and a great-aunt (SC15/64/2). To find if the required sheriff court records have survived, look in the contents list of the relevant SC catalogue for 'Services of Heirs' or 'Record of Services' or similar headings.

9.22 Those of Jedburgh sheriff court have been published in *Services of Heirs, Roxburghshire* (Scottish Record Society). Inquests held in a burgh court may be recorded in the burgh court book (see 13.50). Unless the inquest decision was not retoured, this source is unlikely to provide additional details to those in the retours, but will be in English.

Clare Constat

9.23 The heir of a crown vassal had to have a special retour before he could inherit his ancestor's lands. An heir, whose deceased ancestor was the feudal vassal of a subject-superior, might obtain a document called a precept of clare constat from that superior before he could legally own his ancestor's lands. In this document (usually in Latin), the superior acknowledged that it clearly appeared to him that the heir was the heir of a deceased vassal in specified lands. A precept of clare constat will tell you who the heir and ancestor were, and their relationship. There is no register of such documents, but some survive in private collections (GDs, see 6.19-20), while the instruments of sasine, which followed both them and special retours and repeated the information therein, may be found both in GD collections and in the Register of Sasines (RS — see 10.3 onwards).

Tailzies

9.24 In the Services of Heirs, you may have noticed that an heir may be served as 'Heir of Taillie'. 'Taillie' or 'tailzie' is the Scots form of the word 'entail'. By an Act of the Scottish Parliament 1685, c.22, a landowner was allowed to decide who would succeed to his estate for generations to come by means of a deed of tailzie or entail. An estate was entailed to prevent it going out of the family, either through sale or by marriage. Such a deed had to be recorded in the Register of Tailzies (RT1) and, in the naming of a series of substitute heirs, may include detailed information about the family at that time. For example, in the deed of entail by Major Charles Hamilton of Fairholm, recorded in 1777 (RT1/19, f.265), he names as his heirs, in order, his natural son, a cousin german [first cousin on father's side], another cousin german, his natural daughter, and then six other cousins. Remember that an heir of tailzie usually had to take the surname of the entailer along with the lands, and therefore might have to change his name.

9.25 There is an index to the Register of Tailzies between 1688, when the Register starts, and 1833. This index is a mixture of print and manuscript and lists the granters of the deeds, arranged chronologically under each surname letter. You order by the reference RT1 and the volume number given in the index; which also gives the folio number. The names of the heirs often appear well into a rather lengthy document.

9.26 A digest of the Register of Tailzies between 1688 and 1810, in the

71

Historical Search Room, is of little use to the family historian as it omits the names of the heirs.

9.27 If you are looking for an entry in the Register of Tailzies after 1833, you should go to the Legal Search Room to consult a two-volume manuscript index, referenced RT3/1/1-2 and titled 'Register of Entails'. This indexes the period 1688-1938. Again, the arrangement is alphabetical by first letter of the surname only, then chronological. At the end of each entry, there is a volume and folio number: eg if the entry concludes '114-275', then you order RT1/114 and look up folio 275 therein. Since 1914, the Register contains only disentails.

Beneficium Inventarii

9.28 Until 1847, an heir who took over an ancestor's heritable property could be liable for all the ancestor's debts. However, by an Act of 1695, c.24, an heir who entered by the procedure 'cum beneficio inventarii' was liable only to the extent of the value of the heritable property, provided it was done within a year and a day of the ancestor's death. This procedure is recorded in the Register of Inventories of Heirs Entering Cum Beneficio Inventarii (RD20), which dates from 1696 to 1850. This register is not indexed. A list of the volumes in the Register and the dates they cover is in the RD catalogue. The name of a party is put in the margin at the start of each entry, but this may be the name of either the heir or of the ancestor. You will find in each 'inventory' the names of the heir and his deceased ancestor, sometimes the date of death, and an inventory of the heritable property and the income therefrom.

9.29 The lack of an index limits the usefulness of this record, but there is information in it. Heirs may be cousins. The heirs are not necessarily well-to-do. In 1826, James Davidson, labourer in the parish of Ardclach, was heir to his brother David Davidson, vintner in Nairn (RD20/14, f.153). The next entry in the same volume illustrates how far Scotsmen travelled – Robert Walkinshaw, 'at present in Mexico', was heir to his brother William Walkinshaw, captain in the service of the Honourable East India Company, who died at Ghazapore in the East Indies (RD20/14, f.156).

9.30 Another record which contains information about heirs who were liable for their ancestor's debts is the Register of Adjudications. (See 13.61-63.)

Ultimus Haeres

9.31 Perhaps you are seeking an ancestor who was believed to have died without a known heir. In such a case, the Crown would be the ultimus haeres (last heir) and the heritable and moveable property of the deceased would have been paid into the Exchequer, any lands being sold or granted to a new owner. Fortune hunters should be warned that almost all ultimus haeres estates comprise small amounts of money and that such estates are usually distributed to people who have a moral claim, though not a legal one, such as a relative by marriage who cared for the deceased in his old age. Such claimants would petition for a share of the estate.

9.32 Obviously, you must know the name of the deceased and the approximate date of death.

9.33 Because of legal limitations in the past on those who might succeed on intestacy, the Ultimus Haeres records contain more genealogical information than you might expect. Such limitations were:

a. If a man died childless and intestate, but left a widow, she could claim only part of the estate.

b. An illegitimate person could be succeeded in both heritable and moveable property only by the offspring of his own body. Until 1836, if an illegitimate person had no children, he could not bequeath any property to anyone, unless he had received letters of legitimation from the Crown.

c. There was no succession to or through the mother in either heritable or moveable property, i.e. if a person died intestate and childless, with no relations on his father's side, but with relations on his mother's side including half brothers or sisters, they were excluded and all his property went to the Crown as ultimus haeres. (Since 1855, there has been gradual reform in this legal area.) Thus, many of the petitioners for a gift of an ultimus haeres estate were maternal relations of the deceased and their petitions contain much information about their families.

9.34 Ultimus Haeres records change dramatically in 1834.

Ultimus Haeres before 1834

9.35 Records before 1834 relate almost entirely to the granting of ultimus haeres property to petitioners. Such grants of moveable property were made under the Privy Seal (see 7.17). Those up to 1584 will be found in the printed volumes of the *Register of the Privy Seal*, in which both the deceased and the recipient are indexed. Between 1585 and 1660, you must use the minute books (PS6) to search for such a grant. The originals are ordered by PS1 and the volume number. From 1660, there are two indexes, but only the index from 1782 identifies the gifts of ultimus haeres, indexing both the recipients and estates. Order by the reference PS3 and the volume number. The record of grants of heritable property exists only for the periods 1750-1761 and from 1831 and is unindexed: see the C14 catalogue.

9.36 Petitions for grants of ultimus haeres are preserved among the Exchequer records (E303). The accompanying papers usually include a report advising whether or not a grant should be made. These records are incomplete and unindexed. If you wish to investigate them, look at the list of E303 in the Exchequer catalogue. Some do give detailed family information, eg the papers in the case in 1797 of Lt Col John Rose, who died in Corsica, demonstrate his relationship to a number of people in the Nairn area, including a minister and a bailie, as well as a bricklayer in Glasgow and a book-keeper in Jamaica (E303/6).

Relations of Lt Col John Rose, 1797. (E303/6)

Ultimus Haeres from 1834

9.37 The present procedure for dealing with ultimus haeres cases dates from 1834 and from then there are consistent records. These are in various series, which are explained in the catalogue (E851–870). There is no overall index, but each individual volume is indexed by name of the deceased person, giving the surname and forename only.

9.38 To search, firstly you want to check if the estate of someone you are researching did fall to the Crown. Look at the indexes in the Procedure Books (E851), which give a summary of proceedings relating to every case. Some of these books have two indexes (a separate one for illegitimates). Alternatively, from 1886 you can look at annual alphabetical lists (E869). Once you have established that there was an ultimus haeres case of interest to you, you can look it up in a relevant volume or file of the other series. Particularly useful are the Treasury Reports (E853) that repeat the claims of the petitioners and often include detailed family relationships and histories.

∽ *10* ∽

Owners of Land and Houses

10.1 The previous chapter concerned the transfer of heritable property when the owner died. The ownership, and transfer of ownership, of land and houses is of such importance that records of this are among the earliest to survive. The system of land-holding in Scotland was historically a feudal one. In a feudal system, all land is held of the Crown, either directly or through a subject-superior.

10.2 A grant of land was usually made in a charter by the Crown or subject-superior, but used to require a series of legal documents. You will find examples of the more important ones, which were often in Latin, in Gouldesbrough's *Formulary of Old Scots Legal Documents* (Stair Society). The most important was the instrument of sasine, which until 1858 final-ised all grants of land (including Crown ones) and was essential evidence that change of ownership had taken place. From 1617, such instruments were copied into the Register of Sasines, which is the primary source of information of ownership of property.

Register of Sasines

10.3 Whenever heritable property changed hands or was used as security for a loan, then the document narrating the legal transaction should have been copied ('recorded') into the Register of Sasines. The Register was founded in 1617, though there had been a trial run between 1599 and 1609 called the Secretary's Register, and continues to the present day, when it is be-ing replaced by registration of title. The Secretary's Register is now treated as part of the Register of Sasines and therefore will not be dealt with separately.

10.4 We talk of the Register of Sasines, but in fact there are several registers of sasines. The Secretary's Register was kept in various divisions of the country. Between 1617 and 1868, there was a General Register of Sasines, in which could be recorded documents relating to property in any part of Scotland, and Particular Registers of Sasines (PRS), each for a particular area of the country. Since then, there has been a separate division of the Register for each county. There were separate registers for property in the royal burghs (see 10.16-18).

10.5   The Register of Sasines is particularly useful to genealogists, both because fathers often made gifts of land to their children, and because a document narrating the sale or mortgage of lands may tell you the designation of the granter when he acquired the lands. Therefore you can trace in the Register the development both of families and individuals. Documents therein often refer back to earlier transactions and thus may name persons who died prior to the date of the document.

10.6   After 1780, the Register of Sasines is quite easy to search: before that date, less so.

Register of Sasines 1617-1780

10.7   First, you should know in which part of Scotland your ancestor may have owned land. Unless the property lies within a royal burgh, you should next search the relevant Particular Register. There is a series of indexes but it is an incomplete series. The following table gives the modern county and the equivalent Particular Register and says whether there is a pre-1780 index therefor. The indexes marked with an asterisk have been published, may be purchased from the National Archives of Scotland and should be available through a library.

County	Particular Register of Sasines	Indexes
Aberdeen	Aberdeen till 1660 (RS4-5) Aberdeen and Kincardine from 1661 (RS8)	1599-1660★
Angus (Forfar)	Forfar (RS33-35)	1620-1700★ 1701-1780
Argyll	Argyll etc (RS9-10)	1617-1780★ (now out of print)
Ayr	Ayr etc (RS11-14)	1599-1660★
Banff	Banff (RS15-17)	1600-1780★
Berwick	Berwick etc (RS18-19)	1617-1780★
Bute	Argyll etc (RS9-10)	1617-1780★ (now out of print)

County	Particular Register of Sasines	Indexes
Caithness	Inverness till 1644 (RS36–37)	1606–1780★
	Caithness from 1646 (RS20–21)	
Clackmannan	Stirling etc (RS58–59)	None
Dumfries	Dumfries etc (RS22–23)	1617–1780★
Dunbarton	Argyll etc (RS9–10)	1617–1780★
		(now out of print)
East Lothian		
(Haddington)	Edinburgh etc (RS24–27)	1599–1700★
		1741–1780
Edinburgh City	Edinburgh etc (RS24–27)	1599–1700★
		1741–1780
Fife	Fife and Kinross till 1685	1603–1660★
	Fife from 1685 (RS30–32)	
Glasgow City	Renfrew and Glasgow (RS53–54)	None
Inverness	Inverness etc (RS36–38)	1606–1780★
Kincardine	Kincardine till 1657	1600–1657★
	Aberdeen and Kincardine	
	from 1661 (RS6–8)	
Kinross	Fife and Kinross till 1685	1603–1660★
	Kinross from 1688 (RS30–31, 39)	
Kirkcudbright	Dumfries etc (RS22–23)	1617–1780★
Lanark	Lanark (RS40–42)	1618–1780★
Midlothian		
(Edinburgh)	Edinburgh etc (RS24–27)	1599–1700★
		1741–1780
Moray (Elgin)	Elgin and Nairn (RS28–29)	1617–1780★
Nairn	Elgin and Nairn (RS28–29)	1617–1780★
Orkney	Orkney and Shetland (RS43–47)	1617–1660
Peebles	Roxburgh etc (RS55–57)	None
Perth	Perth (RS48–52)	1601–1609
	Stirling etc (RS58–59)	None
Renfrew	Renfrew and Glasgow (RS53–54)	None
Ross and		
Cromarty	Inverness etc (RS36–38)	1606–1780★
Roxburgh	Roxburgh etc (RS55–57)	None
Selkirk	Roxburgh etc (RS55–57)	None
Shetland	Orkney and Shetland (RS43–47)	1617–1660
Stirling	Stirling etc (RS58–59)	None
Sutherland	Inverness etc (RS36–38)	1606–1780★

County	Particular Register of Sasines	Indexes
West Lothian		
(Linlithgow)	Edinburgh etc (RS24-27)	1599-1700★
		1700-1780
Wigtown	Wigtown (RS60-61)	None

10.8 Determine which Particular Register is the one likely to include your ancestor. If there is an index for that PRS and for that period, obviously you look up that index. These indexes were compiled over several decades and vary in style, but will give the volume and initial folio for each document in which your ancestor appears. All parties who are mentioned as having or having had a heritable right (i.e. not tenants) in the property should be indexed, not just the main parties in the transaction. In some indexes, the volume will be expressed in roman numerals and you will have to convert that into its arabic form. You order by the RS reference number and the volume number, eg RS29/7. Because most of the indexes were compiled before the reference number system was introduced, the RS reference number will not be in the index, but it has usually been annotated at the start of the index. If in doubt check the RS catalogue.

10.9 If there is no index for that Particular Register or period, then look at the RS catalogue for the minute books of that Register. The starting dates of these minute books vary considerably. If there is a minute book for the relevant period, you should order it out by its call number like any other document. The minute books are arranged chronologically by the date of recording. Each minute also states the names of the main parties and lands, and the relevant folios in the volume of the Register. The volume number may not be apparent and should be ascertained, along with its call number, by its dates, from the catalogue.

10.10 If there is no minute book nor index, you have no alternative but to browse through the volumes of the Register itself, which can be a formidable task.

10.11 As the majority of documents in the Register are instruments of sasine, you should familiarise yourself with the structure of this type of deed. Gouldesbrough's *Formulary* contains examples in Latin with English translations. If you are lucky, the copy in the Register will start with an introduction which will tell you to whom the lands were granted, or his name will appear in the margin. In the instrument itself, the first name to be mentioned should be either the grantee or his legal agent. The granter may also have a legal agent (called a 'bailie'). In other words, you must read the document carefully to disentangle who is doing what. In genealogical terms, an added advantage is that witnesses were often relations of the parties. There are two lists of witnesses in an instrument of sasine, one near the end and one about two-thirds through the document at the end of what was known as the precept of sasine.

10.12 As well as searching for your ancestor in the Particular Register for the area in which he owned land, you should also look in the General Register of Sasines, which is indexed up to 1735. From then to 1780, you have to use the minute books which you will find listed in the RS catalogue under the reference number RS62.

Register of Sasines after 1780

10.13 Firstly, decide in which county your ancestor may have owned land. Next, go to the volumes which are stored in the stairwell beneath the stairs which lead to the Historical Search Room. These volumes are the Sasine Abridgements and their indexes. These Abridgements contain printed summaries of all the documents recorded in the Register of Sasines from 1781, chronologically within counties. They are indexed by persons from 1781 to the present and by places from 1781 to 1830 and from 1872 to the present. The earlier abridgements are kept in blocks of years, but more recently each year is separate.

10.14 Select the volume of Abridgements you want for the county and year(s) in which you are interested. Select the equivalent index of persons, which will be in a separate volume. Make sure it is the equivalent index: the covering dates are usually at the top of each page. Look up your ancestor's name in the index of persons, which gives simply the surname and forename, no designation. After the name you will find a number or series of numbers. These numbers are the running numbers of the summaries in the Abridgements. Find the summary which starts with that number. It will be headed by a date and then will tell you, among other things, the names and designations of the new and previous owners and a description of the property. All parties are indexed. If your ancestor's name is a common one and you know the name of the property he owned, you might wish to look up the index of places as well as that of persons to see if any of the summary numbers coincide.

(296)   Jun. 21. 1877.
Disch. by Judicial Factor on the Estates of BALMAUD AND
MORELESS and whole subjects belonging to the deceased
JOHN RUSSELL of Balmund, or forming part of his Trust
Estate,—*disburdening* of Bond (dated 7th Jan., and recorded in
this Register 15th Feb. 1871) for £130, by John Benton resid-
ing at Sheriffhaugh, Parish of Boharm, Banffshire,—(I.) the
House No. 9 NORTH COLLEGE STREET, bounded on the
north by said Street, in Burgh of ELGIN, and (II.) Piece of
ground, with Dwelling House thereon, partly converted into a
Shop, bounded on the north by College Street and on the west
by and extending 56 Feet along Collie Street, in the College of
Elgin, all as described in said Bond (see Minute No. 11, 15th
Feb. 1871). Dated Jun. 1, 1877; with Warrant of Registration
thereon, on behalf of said John Benton.   22. 48.

(297)   Jun. 21. 1877.
Disp. by JOHN BENTON, Farmer, Sheriffhaugh, Banffshire,
to James Thompson Mackay, Jeweller in Elgin,—of Piece of
ground, with Dwelling House thereon, partly converted into a
Shop, bounded on the north by COLLEGE STREET and on
the west by and extending 56 Feet along COLLIE STREET,
being part of the Manse called the MOY MANSE, with Houses,
&c. thereof, in the COLLEGE of ELGIN and Regality of
Spynie. Dated May 23, 1877; with Warrant of Registration
thereon, on behalf of said Grantee.   22. 50.

(298)   Jun. 22. 1877.
Bond for £130, and *Disp.* in security, by DAVID HISLOP,
Mason, residing at Pilmuir near Forres, to Felix Calvert
Mackenzie, Solicitor in Forres,—of Piece of ground (1 Rood 5
perches and 16¼ yards), marked as No. 26 on Plan, bounded on
the south by the Public or Commutation Road from Forres to
Balnageith, on the north by a proposed new Street and on the
east by a proposed new Road, forming part of the land of
PILMUIR, in Parish of Forres, particularly described in Extract
Decr. of Sp. Serv. in favor of Robert Donald Grant, recorded
in this Register 14th Apr. 1871. Dated Nov. 18, 1876; with
Warrant of Registration thereon, on behalf of said Felix Calvert
Mackenzie.   22. 51.

(299)   Jun. 26. 1877.
Not. Instrument, Trustees of the deceased JAMES ROBERT-
SON, sometime Bank Agent in Huntly, thereafter residing in
Church Street there,—of the following subjects in which said
James Robertson was infeft, viz., Piece of land in the MUIR of
GARMOUTH, bounded on the south by the High Road from
Garmouth to Elgin, in Parish of Speymouth;—on Extract of
Trust Disp. and Settl., dated 6th Aug. 1859, by said James
Robertson and his wife Isabella Kirkwood Neilson Mackray or
Robertson, and two Codicils thereto by him, all recorded in
Books of Council and Session 7th Feb. 1877, containing a Gen.
Convey. by him; and another Writ; with Warrant of Registra-
tion thereon, on behalf of said Trustees.   22. 54.

Excerpt from Sasine Abridgements for Elgin and Forres.

10.15 The summary in the Abridgements may give you all the information you require, but if you wish to study the full text of the document in the Register of Sasines, take note of the numbers given at the end of the summary. You will then have to go back to the Historical Search Room to find the call numbers from the RS catalogue and to order out the Sasine volume. If the number at the end of the summary is preceded by the letters GR, then the document will be in the General Register of Sasines (RS3); if by the letters PR, then it will be in the Particular Register of Sasines which includes that county (see list at 10.7); and if it is preceded by no letters, then it will be in one of the post-1868 county divisions of the Register. As usual the first number is the volume number, and the second number the folio number, and you order by the RS number and the volume number. For example, a Clackmannan abridgement dated 'Dec.28, 1802' ends 'PR.37.333'. The Particular Register of Sasines for Stirling and Clackmannan is RS59 and you order out RS59/37. A Glasgow abridgement in 1881 ends with the reference '1064.174'. You find from the list in the RS catalogue that the Glasgow call number is RS102 and order out RS102/1064.

Burgh Registers of Sasines

10.16 Each royal burgh was entitled to have its own burgh register of sasines. If your ancestor owned property in a royal burgh, then the record of that ownership will probably not be in the General or a Particular Register of Sasines, though it is wise to check them as well as the burgh register. Remember that many of these burghs lay within much smaller boundaries than they do today. The National Archives of Scotland holds the registers of sasines of the burghs of Aberdeen, Annan★, Anstruther Wester, Arbroath, Auchtermuchty★, Ayr, Banff, Brechin, Burntisland★, Crail, Cullen★, Culross, Cupar, Dingwall, Dornoch, Dumbarton, Dumfries, Dunbar, Dundee, Dunfermline, Dysart★, Earlsferry, Edinburgh★, Elgin, Falkland, Forfar★, Forres, Fortrose★, Haddington, Hawick, Inverbervie★, Inverkeithing, Inverness, Inverurie, Irvine, Jedburgh, Kinghorn★, Kintore★, Kirkcaldy★, Kirkcudbright, Kirkwall, Lanark, Lauder, Linlithgow, Lochmaben★, Montrose, Nairn★, Newburgh★, New Galloway, North Berwick★, Paisley★, Peebles, Perth, Pittenweem, Queensferry★, Renfrew, Rothesay, Rutherglen★, St Andrews, Sanquhar, Selkirk, Stirling, Stranraer, Tain★, Whithorn★, Wigtown★. The Glasgow burgh register and the Aberdeen and Dundee pre-1809 registers are kept by Glasgow City Archives, Aberdeen City Archives and City of Dundee Archive and Record Centre respectively (addresses in Appendix A).

10.17 The commencement dates of the Burgh Registers of Sasines held by the National Archives of Scotland vary tremendously from 1602 (Dysart) to 1881 (Forres). They were discontinued at various dates between 1926 and 1963 and thereafter all properties appear in the General Register of Sasines. The burgh registers marked with an asterisk in 10.16 have type-script indexes, but (save for Rutherglen, which covers 1631-1777) none of these start before 1809 and they index only those who are being granted ownership. If your ancestor lived in one of the asterisked burghs after 1809, look up the relevant index. Each index entry gives a volume and folio number, but to find the call number, you have to consult the burgh catalogue (B), eg in the index to the Burgh Register of Sasines of Whithorn, there is an entry for Peter Houl, soldier in 7th Hussars, in 1815. The volume is 1, the folio 100, and you order out B71/2/1 and look up folio 100. As Whithorn, like most burghs, has more than one series of its Register of Sasines, you must make certain by checking the date that you are ordering the volume from the correct series.

10.18 To search for your ancestor otherwise in a Burgh Register of Sasines look up the introduction to the Burgh catalogue (B) to find the number that relates to that particular burgh (eg Culross is B12). Look up the pages under that number to find the dates of that Burgh Register. Check to see if there is a manuscript index or minute book, which you may consult. If there is not, you will have to go directly to a volume of the Burgh Register of Sasines, some of which have a contents list or index in the volume.

Notarial Protocol Books

10.19 If you are seeking an ancestor who owned heritable property before the setting up of the Register of Sasines in 1617 or before the start of the burgh registers of sasines, or if you cannot find an entry in the Register of Sasines before 1660, you might investigate the Notarial Protocol books. These were record books kept by notaries, who were lawyers officially authorised to draw up certain legal documents, including instruments of sasine. Their books contain copies or notes of the documents they compiled. Not all these books were kept to the standard one might expect in a public register.

10.20 If your ancestor owned property in a royal burgh (see 10.16), look up the B catalogue at the list of records under the name of that burgh to see if they include any protocol books (not all do). There you will find the reference number and covering dates of each protocol book. A handful are indexed, but most are not, and therefore you must simply order out the book which covers the approximate date and browse through it.

10.21 If your ancestor owned property anywhere else, go to the catalogue of Notarial records (NP). This includes a topographical guide, mainly under the names of counties, which will provide you with the reference numbers of the books of notaries who worked in different parts of Scotland: eg if you look up Shetland, you will find only one notary who operated there between 1576 and 1615, the reference number of his protocol book being NP1/36. None of these books is indexed, but the catalogue notes those that have been printed by the Scottish Record Society and those for which there are abstracts. These abstracts are referenced RH2/1/16-26 (see the RH2 catalogue). You may find the abstracts and printed versions, both of which are translated into English, easier to read than the originals, and the printed books are indexed.

Crown Grants of Land

10.22 If you think your ancestor was granted lands by a Crown charter, there are three other records you should examine – those of the Great Seal, Privy Seal and Signatures. The copies of charters in the Register of the Privy Seal and the Signatures were, in effect, drafts of those in the Great Seal Register. The Signatures have the advantage that they are in English while the Great and Privy Seal records are in Latin. We suggest that you search first in the Great Seal Register, and then search in the Privy Seal Register or Signatures if the charter is not in the Great Seal Register or you require the English version in the Signatures.

Great Seal

10.23 The record of the charters issued under the Great Seal dates from 1314 and is published up to 1668 in the eleven volumes of the *Register of the Great Seal of Scotland* (or *Registrum Magni Sigilli Regum Scotorum*, or RMS for short). As volume 1 of the RMS was compiled from a variety of sources and few people are likely to trace their ancestry back to the fourteenth century, the following comments relate to the record from 1424, when volume 2 of the RMS starts.

10.24 Each volume of the RMS is indexed. The charters (in summary form) and indexes are in Latin until 1651. If you are looking for a Crown charter to your ancestor up to 1668, look up the 'Index Nominum' in the volume of the RMS which covers the likely date. In these indexes up to 1651, forenames are in Latin or are abbreviated and designations are in Latin. Each entry in the index is followed by a number – this is the running number of the summaries in the volume. These summaries are quite detailed, but if you want to see the original, take note of the numbers at the end of the summary, the roman number being the volume number and the arabic the running number (not the folio number) of the charters in the original record.

10.25 If the roman number is preceded by the letters 'PR' (which stands for 'Paper Register') order out by the reference C3 and the volume number (converted into arabic). Otherwise, the call reference is C2 and the volume number, but, as many of the volumes are in two bulky parts, you should look at the Chancery catalogue under C2 to check which part you should order. For example, in the RMS, volume 4, you have found an entry concerning a family named Leslie, and at the end of the entry you read 'xxxiv.582'. If you look in the catalogue, you find that volume 34 is in two parts and no.582 is in the second part; and therefore you should order out C2/34 part 2.

10.26 If you are seeking your ancestor in this record from 1668, look at the several typed indexes to the various series of Great Seal records. The indexes which deal with grants of lands are a 4-volume index to the Register of the Great Seal itself 1668-1919, an index to the Paper Register 1668-1852 and an index to the Principality Register 1716-1913. The introductory notes to these indexes explain the differences between the records. Each index gives the name and designation of the grantee, the lands granted, the date, and the volume and either folio or running number of the charter in that volume. If the charter is in the Great Seal Register, order by C2, the volume number and the part number if the volume is in two parts (the catalogue will tell you). If it is in the Paper Register, order by C3 and the volume number. If it is in the Principality Register, check the introduction to the index to find out the call number (mostly C16) and order by that and the volume number. The Paper Register continues after 1852 but contains no further grants of land.

Privy Seal

10.27 How to search the Privy Seal has been described in 7.17. Use the printed and indexed *Register of the Privy Seal of Scotland* up to 1584, and the minute books thereafter. The call number up to 1660 is PS1 and the volume number. After 1660, the call number of the 'Latin Register' in which grants of land are recorded is PS2 and the volume number. The only indexes to PS2 are a rather variable set of manuscript indexes between 1660 and 1705, which you order out by PS7/2.

Signatures

10.28 The surviving Signatures date from 1607 to 1847. There is a 2-volume index which tells you the name of the grantee, the lands, the date, and the box and running number or volume and folio number of the signatures. Order by SIG1 and the box and running number or SIG2 and the volume number.

Original Charters and Other Writs

10.29 If you have been unable to find a grant of land to your ancestor in the Crown records or registers of sasines or protocol books, you should investigate original documents, particularly before 1660. After that date, the Register of Sasines is complete enough to be reliable.

10.30 The main source for original legal documents in the NAS is the Gifts and Deposits series (see 6.19-20). Check the inventories of GDs which concern likely families or relevant parts of Scotland. A few GDs include cartularies, which list grants given by subject-superiors.

10.31 Other series of original documents may be found in the inventories of the RH class of records. Particularly useful are RH9/15, which contains miscellaneous writs of lands in Orkney and Shetland, arranged by placenames, and RH6-8, which contain miscellaneous charters and other writs.

10.32 The writs in RH6 date between 1142 and 1600. They are calendared in 15 volumes ('Calendar of Charters', on the open shelves) and indexed in 8 volumes. All parties, including witnesses, are indexed. The index gives each personal name and designation and the running number in the calendar. RH6 has one running number throughout. The entry in the calendar may be enough for you and it is in English, but if you wish to see the original, order by RH6 and the running number.

10.33 The writs in RH7 date from 1601 to 1830. As they are not individually listed, there is no easy way of identifying the persons involved in them, but, as they are arranged in strict chronological order, if you are looking for a writ of a particular date, you can order out the box which includes writs for that year by the reference RH7 and the box number you find in the catalogue.

10.34 The writs in RH8 are dated between 1700 and 1800 and are arranged by name of the grantee. There is a two-volume inventory. If you wish to see a document, order by RH8 and the running number in the margin of the inventory.

Valuation Rolls

10.35 Information about the ownership and sometimes tenancy of land and houses was often gathered because of taxes on the value of such properties. From 1855, the Valuation Rolls (VR) themselves supply this information consistently for the whole of Scotland. Before that date, records of such information for tax purposes are occasional.

Valuation Rolls before 1855

10.36 Valuation rolls before 1855 are sporadic and inconsistent. As the purpose of such a record was to record the value of lands, in some instances that is all that is given and the names of proprietors and occupiers are simply omitted. Still, however imperfect for your purposes these records are, you may wish to take pot luck with them. If you do find the name of a proprietor you are seeking, you may be led on to search a more productive record, such as the Register of Sasines or a GD collection.

10.37 Firstly, look in the part of the Exchequer catalogue (E) which includes the reference E106. Here are listed valuation rolls, arranged by counties and dated variously between 1643 and 1835. Published versions are noted. If you order out a roll, you will discover that it is arranged by parishes. Sometimes no personal names are given; sometimes only the biggest landowners are named, eg 'Robert Arbuthnot of Katerlane for himselff and remnant heritors' (E106/1/2); but occasionally tenants are named in the description of lands, eg 'That part of Old Mains posest by Jas Forsyth' (E106/14/2). *A Directory of Land Ownership in Scotland c.1770* by Lorretta R Timperley (Scottish Record Society) is largely based on these valuation rolls for 1771 and is indexed.

10.38 Next, if you are interested in early nineteenth century valuation rolls, look at the Inland Revenue catalogue (IRS). It lists land tax or valuation rolls for the following counties and dates before 1855. Within counties, the arrangement is by parishes.

> Aberdeen, 1847-57 (IRS4/1)
> Ayr, c1837-1839 (IRS4/2)
> Banff, 1836-1837 (IRS4/3)
> Dumfries, 1827 (IRS4/S)
> Fife, 1837 (IRS4/7)
> Lanark, 1837-41 (IRS3/11) and 1846-60 (IRS4/8)
> Midlothian and Edinburgh City, 1814, 1837-71 (IRS4/9)
> Roxburgh, 1842 (IRS4/12)
> Stirling, 1831 (IRS4/14)

Again, the information supplied varies. You will probably be given the names of the proprietors or most of them. They may be listed alphabetically, showing the parishes in which they owned land. If you are lucky, you may find the names not only of proprietors, but also of tenants who paid land tax. Watch out for later annotations, of unspecified date, which may confuse the information.

10.39 There are some valuation rolls among the Gifts and Deposits. Many can be located using the NAS's electronic catalogue. Other GD collections not yet on this system will require more hunting.

10.40 If your ancestor owned property in a royal burgh, then these valuation rolls will not be useful. A separate collection of land tax was made within each royal burgh from the inhabitants thereof. Of the royal burgh records at present within the NAS, only Dunbar, Inverkeithing, Jedburgh, Linlithgow, North Berwick and Peebles include cess or stent rolls which list the inhabitants liable to pay tax, before 1855. These records sometimes state the trade of the inhabitant, but rarely the property owned. Look them up in the B catalogue to find the dates covered and the reference number.

10.41 Similar valuations were made of each parish by the heritors and some survive in the Heritors Records (HR). The heritors were the landowners in each parish who until 1925 were responsible for the maintenance of church, manse, school and (until 1845) the poor of the parish. The money to pay for these outlays was raised from the landowners themselves by assessment on the value of their lands. Records of such assessments survive for a minority of parishes and are mainly nineteenth century. The heritors are always named in them, their lands not always. If you know the name of the parish in which your ancestor may have owned land, look it up in the index of parishes, which is part of the HR catalogue. The index will supply the reference number of the parish, eg Dunbar is HR69. You then look in the catalogue at the list of records under that reference number for any assessment rolls or book or lists. (For example, Dunbar has assessment rolls between 1773 and 1904 – HR69/10/4). As landowners could reclaim from their tenants half of the sum they paid towards poor relief, these assessment rolls very occasionally include the names of tenants with or without the names of their farms. Lands in a royal burgh were usually assessed and paid in a block, without naming the property owners.

10.42 The names of property owners may also be found in the tax records referenced E326 and 327, discussed in 15.5-11. If your ancestor owned or occupied a property in Midlothian, including Edinburgh, between 1803 and 1812, you should find him in the Property Tax records (E327/ 78-121) or Small House or Cottage Tax records (E327/122-127).

Valuation Rolls since 1855

10.43 The Lands Valuation (Scotland) Act 1854 established a uniform valuation of lands and houses throughout Scotland. Separate valuation rolls were to be compiled annually for every burgh and county, listing every house or piece of ground, along with the names and designations of the proprietor, tenant and occupier, and its value. However, one proviso, unfortunate from our point of view, was that the occupiers of property which was let at less than £4 per year did not need to be named. With that exception, if your ancestor owned or occupied property in Scotland since 1855, his name should appear in the Valuation Rolls. Only the heads of households would be named.

10.44 Look at the catalogue of the Valuation Rolls (VR) for the burgh or county in which you think your ancestor owned or occupied property. The burghs are listed first, then the counties and cities. There is no persons index, but sometimes there are indexes of streets and place-names – these are noted in the catalogue. Within the annual volume for a county, the arrangement may be alphabetical by parishes. Ayr county is divided into Carrick, Cunningham and Kyle, but a list of parishes in each of these districts is placed at the start of the list of Ayr county rolls. Lanark county is divided into Upper, Middle and Lower wards.

10.45 Searching for a particular person, even if you know the likely address, can be painstaking. If you are searching in a well-populated part of the country, there may be several volumes for each year through which you have to search. The arrangement within volumes may not always seem logical and is not necessarily consistent year-by-year. The entries for one street will often be dispersed. Street numbers and names can both have been changed over the years.

10.46 Edinburgh and Glasgow VRs are particularly awkward to search. Glasgow, up to 1909, is valued within the parishes of Glasgow, Govan and Barony. An index of streets in 1875-6 is available in the Historical Search Room. As it shows the parish each street is in, it can be used for other years to identify the volume you should order out. Edinburgh is divided by parishes up to 1895, and thereafter by wards. A preliminary study of nineteenth century large-scale Ordnance Survey maps and city directories is recommended, perhaps in combination with a visit to the Edinburgh Room in the Edinburgh Central Library. The Edinburgh Valuation Rolls since 1912 have street indexes which are available in the Legal Search Room. The annual Post Office Directories for Edinburgh and Glasgow often included a note of the ward number in their streets index; the NAS library holds copies of some of these.

10.47 The Local Government Finance Act 1988 introduced the Community Charge for domestic ratepayers. The new tax replaced the system described in paragraphs 10.43–10.46 and the Valuation Rolls that continue after 1 April 1989 list only those premises which are liable for non-domestic rates. They are therefore of little or no use to family historians.

Community Charge Registers 1989 to 1993

10.48 The Community Charge for domestic ratepayers was introduced into Scotland on 1 April 1989. It was a tax on individuals rather than on property, which is why it was soon nicknamed the 'Poll Tax'. All adults aged 18 or over had to pay unless they were exempt (eg because they were in prison).

10.49 NAS holds microfiche copies of all the Community Charge Registers for Scotland, but these are closed for 30 years. The registers are arranged by region, and within that by district, then ward, then street. If your ancestor was eligible to pay the Community Charge, he will be listed at the address where he was registered, together with his date of birth. Full-time students living away from home were registered at their study address rather than at their parents' address. The registers occasionally give alternative correspondence addresses for individuals, and sometimes specify whether someone was the property's owner or a tenant.

10.50 The Community Charge lasted until 1993, when the Local Government Finance Act 1992 replaced it with a tax based on property value: the Council Tax. NAS holds microfiche copies of the Council Tax valuation lists, but these are not useful for family history because they do not list residents or owners of the properties – just addresses and Council Tax valuation bands.

Electors

10.51 As, until 1918, ownership of heritable property above a certain value was a qualification for the right to vote in a parliamentary election, your land-owning ancestor may appear in the records described in 26.2-6.

11

Tenants and Crofters

11.1 The chances are that your ancestors were tenants rather than owners of where they stayed. Since 1855, the Valuation Rolls, described in 10.35 onwards, record most, though not all, tenants in Scotland and you will look for your more recent ancestors in that record. Unfortunately, before 1855, no consistent record was kept of tenancies. Also, records that were kept and that have survived are largely of tenancies of farms. Records of ownership of property, described in Chapter 10, often contain incidental references to tenancies, sometimes identifying a piece of land by the name of its tenant. Between 1832 and 1918, registers of voters state if the voter was a tenant and of what property (see Chapter 26). This chapter will deal with other records which you might examine if your ancestor was a tenant, especially a tenant-farmer. Remember that many people, such as farm workers, would be neither tenant nor owner of where they stayed.

Rentals and Tacks

11.2 A tenancy was agreed by a document known as a tack (lease), but there was no register of tacks, and, after a tenancy had run its course, no legal necessity to preserve the tack. However, some have survived in private papers, as have rentals, in which many landlords, particularly big landowners, listed their tenanted properties. Rentals, like the older valuation rolls, may sometimes just name the lands and not the occupiers, and, though they generally name tenants, these will only be the heads of household and will commonly omit any designation.

11.3 Rentals and tacks are records of private individuals. You need to know which family owned the property of which your ancestor may have been a tenant, and then to find out if the records of that family have survived. This leads us again to the GDs, described in 6.19-20. In most of the larger GDs, there will be a separate section for estate papers, which should include any records of tenancies. The Breadalbane papers (GD112) have a particularly good series of rentals and tacks for north Perthshire and part of Argyll dating from the sixteenth century.

11.4 If the GDs fail you, you might wish to check for rentals in certain public records.

11.5 The Commissioners of Crown Estates (CR) also held records of Glenlivet and Fochabers. These two estates belonged to the Duke of Gordon, but fell to the Crown in lieu of death duties in 1937. Look in the CR catalogue under CR6 and CR8. There are rentals between 1770 and 1890. As the Duke of Gordon's own papers are also in the NAS (GD44), you have a fair chance of finding a reference to an ancestor who was a Gordon tenant.

11.6 Estates forfeited because of their owners' support for the Jacobite cause in 1745 were administered by the Barons of Exchequer and records of that administration are preserved in the Exchequer records. To see if these estates include one relevant to your research, look in the inventory of the Forfeited Estates papers (E700-788) at the contents list under 'Particular Management' or the location list under county and parish. There are rentals of all the estates (with contents lists by name of the forfeited owners) for the period 1747-76 under the reference E707 and rentals of particular estates under the reference number for that estate. These rentals include some 'judicial rentals' which are records of statements by tenants about their tenancies and which supply slightly more information than an ordinary rental. There is also a published list of tenants of farms on some of these estates in 1755 in *Statistics of the Annexed Estates* (copies may be purchased from the NAS).

11.7 There are also some rentals in the RH series. Look in the catalogue for RH9, which lists most of these miscellaneous rentals, and for RH11, which lists a few rentals among local court records.

11.8 Rentals provide an example of how similar records can be found in a variety of record groups. For instance, say your ancestors were tenants on the estate of Callendar near Falkirk in the eighteenth century. You will find rentals dated 1717 in the RH series (RH11/10/1), dated 1748 in the Forfeited Estates paper (E761/1/3), and dated 1785-91 in the Forbes of Callendar muniments (GD171/2100), now transmitted to The History Research Centre, Callendar House, Falkirk.

11.9 Estate records often include plans of the estate, on which the names of tenant might be annotated on their piece of land. Such plans in the NAS are in the Register House Plans series (RHP), described in 20.3. Search the electronic catalogue for the name of the farm itself, or for the parish in which the relevant estate, farm or other property lay.

11.10 Tenants at the end of the eighteenth century may be found in the tax record discussed in 15.5-9, including a useful record of tenant-farmers in the record of taxes on work-horses (E326/10).

Tenants in Trouble

11.11 Records of some tenants have survived because they failed to pay their rent or refused to leave at the end of their tenancy when the landlord wished to re-acquire the property. The landlord might then pursue the tenant in a court of law. Until 1747, this would be most likely a local court (see Chapter 13) which might well be the landlord's own court. After 1747, the court would be a sheriff or burgh court (see 13.38-42 and 13.50). The records of such cases are generally intermingled with those of other court cases, are not indexed and therefore may require a lot of searching. Separate records of such cases in the sheriff courts exist only from the later nineteenth century, when information about tenancies is more easily obtained from the Valuation Rolls. However, you may wish to investigate these records.

11.12 Look in the contents list of the catalogue of the relevant sheriff court for 'Register of Sequestrations for Rent'. If there is no such entry, look up 'Register of Sequestrations', as that may include sequestrations for rent. These records most commonly start in 1867, but some start later, while Cupar (SC20/11) starts in 1839. As a separate entity, records of cases of removal of tenants only occur in the twentieth century – look for 'Summary Removing Court Books' in the catalogue – except for the Dundee court where they start in 1885 (SC45/10).

Crofters

11.13 Crofters are a class of agricultural tenant, for the most part in the Highlands and Islands. Records about crofters postdate the Valuation Rolls, but may provide a record of low-rent tenants omitted from the Valuation Rolls. References to people who lived or worked on the land might appear in the files of the Department of Agriculture and Fisheries and it

```
                              Police Station,
                       BARRA. 18th July, 1908.


Sir,

              SQUATTERS  ON  VATERSAY.
          ───────────────────────────

       I beg to report that after visiting the Island of
Sandray, as separately reported, I proceeded from there
on this date to Vatersay Island, and found in all 32
Squatter's huts, situated as follows:-

       22 around head of Vatersay bay, immediately below
Vatersay house occupied by Mr Macdonald, Farmer; 4 at
Eorisdale; 3 at Aoidh; and 3 at Caolis.

       Accompanied by P.C. Macdonald, I visited each of
these and found them occupied as follows:-

   1.       Mary Campbell or Campbell, wife of Duncan Campbell,
         from Kentangaval, Barra- now undergoing sentence
         of 2 months imprisonment for Breach of Interdict,
         and their three sons, Neil, 19 years: Alexander,
         18 years; and Michael, 12 years.
            She told me her husband went there in the Autumn
         of 1906, erected the wooden hut in which I found her,
         and cultivated following spring about an acre of land
         on which he planted potatoes.  This piece of land is
         now under corn, and about another acre cultivated last
         spring and now under potatoes.  She also told me she
         has a pet lamb and 2 cows now grazing on Vatersay.

   2.       Mary Ann Campbell or Sinclair, wife of John
         Sinclair, fisherman, from Mingulay- now undergoing
         sentence of 2 months imprisonment for Breach of
         Interdict, and their 4 children, Andrew, 5 years:
         Peter, 4 years: Allan Joseph, 2 years: and Mary,
         11 months.
```

Report on Vatersay land raiders, 1908 (AF67/137)

may be worth investigating the AF files if your ancestor fell into this category.

11.14 The records of the Royal Commission on the Highlands and Islands, 1883, are an important source of information about crofters. Look up the catalogue of the Department of Agriculture and Fisheries (AF) for AF50. There are two sets of relevant returns, AF50/7 and AF50/8. AF50/7 consists of returns, bound by counties, of crofters. Within the county volume, the arrangement is alphabetical by estate. The information given includes the name of the township and/or croft, the name of each tenant, the number of families on the croft and the number of persons habitually residing in the croft. AF50/8 consists of unbound returns of cottars, who are tenants of cottages without land attached. These returns are by estate, and, as well as giving the name of each cottar, specify their occupation or means of subsistence, eg 'supported by a son at sea – a Sailor' (AF50/8/2).

Land Court

11.15 If your ancestor was a crofter after 1886 or a small agricultural tenant anywhere in Scotland after 1912, you might want to look at the records of the Scottish Land Court (LC) which has jurisdiction in certain matters relating to these landholdings. First read the introduction to the LC catalogue. Most of the Land Court records are arranged by county. The records of each county include landholders books and court rolls. Particularly before 1912, the cases are predominantly for valuation of fair rent. Both the landholders books and the court rolls are indexed by the name of the applicant, i.e. the tenant or crofter. This gives this record a searching advantage over the Valuation Rolls in respect of tenants who applied to the Land Court. The applications are closed for 75 years.

∽ *12* ∽

Other Legal Transactions

12.1 During his lifetime, your ancestor may have been engaged in a variety of legal transactions, which required documents which bear his name – bonds, contracts of sale, contracts of partnership, and so forth. While there was generally no public compulsion to preserve such records of private enterprise, many such documents have survived. Your problem is to find any which relate to your ancestor.

12.2 Fortunately, there was and is a type of record which was created for the purpose of preserving such legal documents (or 'deeds'), though only if the parties wished. In the sixteenth century, it became the practice for most courts of law to have a register of deeds, in which such documents were copied, either simply to ensure their preservation or to facilitate a legal action grounded on the deed. The original document was also often kept by the court. Up to 1809, any court had power to register deeds. After that date, only the Court of Session, sheriff courts and royal burgh courts had the power. If you are looking for a deed which you hope will have been copied into a register of deeds, you will need to look at both the register compiled in the Court of Session and the registers of any courts which had jurisdiction where your ancestor lived or was engaged in business. Any legal document might be copied into these registers. Deeds are arranged therein by date of registration, not the date of the deed. Some deeds have been registered years after the date of the deed. Thus, in seeking a deed which you hope has been registered, you may have to search several records and a longish date period, often without the aid of indexes.

Books of Council and Session

12.3 The register attached to the Court of Session is known both as the 'Books of Council and Session' and, simply, 'The Register of Deeds' (RD). Indexing of this huge Register is patchy. We will consider its accessibility before and after 1660.

The Register of Deeds before 1660

12.4 While the Register of Deeds is officially regarded as starting in 1554, it was not a tidy start. Deeds had been previously registered in other Court of Session court books and some continued to be so. There are calendars available of deeds in the Acta Dominorum Concilii 1501-1514 (CS5), Acta Dominorum Concilii et Sessionis 1532-1559 (CS6) and Acts and Decreets 1542-1581 (indexed, CS7). Order by the CS reference and volume number.

12.5 There is a Calendar of Deeds in the Register of Deeds itself for the period between 1554 and 1595, in a series of volumes with a lot of date overlap. These are partly indexed in separate volumes. Order the Register volume containing the deed by RD1 and the volume number.

12.6 Between 1596 and 1660, there are no calendars or indexes, and thus, to search the Register of Deeds, you will have to use its minute books. Before 1660, there are five series of minute books, partly concurrent. Look up the Register of Deeds catalogue under the reference RD6. Each of the five series appears under a name: 'Scott', 'Gibson', 'Hay', 'Dounie', and 'Brown', the names of the clerks' offices which compiled the Register. Order out the minute books which cover the date period you are searching. Each minute book is arranged by date of registration and gives that date, an abbreviation of the type of document, and the surnames only of the principal parties, expressed as if parties in a legal dispute. If you find a promising entry, order out the RD1 volume that covers the date and which, according to the catalogue, bears the same office name as the minute book. For example, when you are looking for an ancestor named Kincaid, you find in a Hay minute book under the date 'undecimo decemb: 1639' (undecimo being Latin for eleven) an entry 'Gray qr Kincaid – disch' ('qr' is short for 'contra'). Therefore you order out RD1/524, which, the catalogue tells you, is the Hay volume covering November 1639 to July 1640. In this volume, the dates of registration are placed prominently and the names of the parties are placed in the margins, and therefore the entry is easy to find. The deed is a discharge by Jean Kincaid, relict of umquhile Mr Thomas Gray, advocate, of payment in terms of their marriage contract.

The Register of Deeds from 1661

12.7 From 1661 to 1811, the Register of Deeds was compiled in three separate but concurrent series, known as 'DAL', 'DUR', and 'MACK', which are

Rob Roy's contract with the Duke of Montrose (RD14/52).

abbreviated forms of the names of the three clerks' offices which compiled the Register, i.e. Dalrymple, Durie and Mackenzie. As there is no content distinction between the three offices, any deed might be registered by any of them and you have to search all three. Fortunately, the indexes are to all three series in one.

12.8 From 1661-1696, there are printed annual indexes. Copies may be obtainable through your local library and may be purchased from the NAS. Indexes have also been prepared for the years 1697-1702, 1705-7 and 1714-15, but are available for sale only on microfiche. The style of these indexes varies, but all provide the name and designation of each party, and the volume and folio number of the deed. All principal parties are indexed. To order out a volume of the Register, if the volume number in the index is preceded by DAL, order by RD2 and the volume number; if DUR, order by RD3 and the volume number; if MACK, order by RD4 and the volume number. Occasionally, a deed has been omitted from the volume of the Register but has survived among the original documents kept as 'warrants' of the Register. If the index says 'warrant' instead of a volume number, order by RD12 (for DAL), RD13 (for DUR), or RD14 (for MACK), a number for the year (1 for 1661, 2 for 1662 and so on up to 151 for 1811), and the warrant number, eg RD13/33/no.547. For warrants after 1811, you order by RD15, the year number, which is 1 for 1812, 2 for 1813 and so on, and the warrant number, if you know it. If you want to order an original deed, but do not know its warrant number, you can order by the RD number, the year number (as before), the month and day of registration, and the names of the parties.

12.9 A regular series of indexes starts again in 1770. Up to that date there are modern indexes for 1750-52 and a manuscript index for 1765. Thus, most of the eighteenth-century Register of Deeds is unindexed.

12.10 To search for a deed registered in the unindexed years, you have again to use minute books, of which there are three concurrent series to search: DAL (RD7/1), DUR (RD7/2) and MACK (RD7/3). Look at the catalogue for the reference numbers of minute books covering specific dates. Again, you have to browse through the minute books, all three sets, each arranged chronologically by date of registration, to find an entry which may seem to be relevant. The later minute books state the forenames as well as surnames of parties, which helps. For example: you will find in a DAL minute book (RD7/1/5) on 30 March 1714, an entry 'Cont of Mar Arnot & Spalden', which leads you to the volume of the Register referenced RD2/103/2, in which you will find the date of registration at the top of each page and the names of parties at the head of each deed; and thus you find the contract of marriage, dated in 1694, between Archibald Arnott, chirurgeon apothecary in Dundee, and Catherine Spalding, daughter of Mr John Spalding, minister in Dundee. In a MACK minute book (RD7/3/10) on 3 July 1750, you find 'Latter Will George Brodie to Katherine Brodie'. The will, which is in RD4/176/2, does not appear to be in the Commissary Court records, and is the will of a soldier, signed at Breda in 1748, bequeathing his property to his four sisters.

12.11 Annual contemporary indexes have been compiled to the Register of Deeds since 1770. Their main disadvantage is that they index granters only. Alongside the name and brief designation of the granter, there is the name of the grantee, the type of deed, dates of deed and registration and the volume and folio number. In the RD2, 3 and 4 series, often one volume number is allocated to one calendar year, while the amount of deeds in that year requires two volumes, parts 1 and 2. Thus when, in the volume column of the index, you find (eg) an entry '2/240' with 'Dur' in an adjacent column, you order out RD3/240/2. From 1812 on, you will be glad to hear, there are no longer the three separate offices, and the Register of Deeds exists in one series: order by RD5 and the volume number. There is a set of these annual indexes up to 1850 in the Historical Search Room. You must go down to the Legal Search Room to search the indexes from 1851 and then return to the Historical Search Room to order out the requisite volume of the Register.

12.12 A common entry in the minute book is 'pro' for 'protest', a particular step in some actions for debt and often entered in registers of deeds. Protests are not included in the post-1770 indexes, and therefore to search for them, you will need to continue to use the minute books. From 1812, there is a separate Register of Protests (RD17) that you search by means of its minute books (RD18).

Sheriff Court Registers of Deeds

12.13 Extending your search for a deed to the registers of deeds kept by lesser courts may not be simple. There are a variety of courts and hardly any indexes. The next most important registers of deeds are those of the sheriff courts. Not all sheriff courts kept a register of deeds, but there is at least one for each sheriffdom. As usual, look first in the catalogue of the records of a relevant sheriff court to see if it has a register of deeds. These registers of deeds vary tremendously in their earliest date and in how well they have survived. The earliest surviving is Perth (SC49), which starts in 1570. The majority of sheriff courts have, as well as the registers of deeds themselves, minute books and warrants thereof, but not necessarily all three concurrently. For example, the Wigtown sheriff court (SC19) has minute books from 1636, warrants from 1690, but no register until 1809. More commonly, minute books post-date their register and its warrants. From 1809, these registers were kept in a consistent form and such indexes as exist mainly date from then, but largely this record is unindexed. Check first to see if there is an index for your sheriff court and date or if a relevant volume of the register has an internal contents list or whether there is a contemporary minute book. Otherwise, you will have to sift through a register or box of original warrants of relevant date. The sheriff courts also have separate registers of protests from 1809 (some earlier), which are unindexed.

Burgh Registers of Deeds

12.14 The NAS holds registers of deeds for a number of the royal burghs. Look in the B catalogue at the contents list of the records of the burgh where your ancestor was to see if there is a register of deeds. The dates of these vary considerably, starting with Edinburgh in 1561 (B22/8). They continue into the twentieth century. Very few have minute books. If you are lucky, the appropriate volume may include an index or contents list. If not, look for the names of the parties in the margin beside or at the head of each entry in the register. A few burghs kept not only a register of deeds but also concurrently a register of probative writs, which was a class of deed. If so, that should also be consulted.

Commissary Courts Registers of Deeds

12.15 If you are searching for a deed before 1809, you might look at the Commissary Court registers of deeds. Between them, they cover the whole of Scotland, except that the Wigtown court has no register of deeds, while for Aberdeen and the Isles only warrants survive. Look at 8.6 to find out which commissary court(s) served the county in which your ancestor lived. Then look at its (or their) contents list(s) in the CC catalogue. Look carefully: there may be a separate register of probative writs; there may or may not be minute books. Many of these registers have gaps; if so, look also at the warrants of these registers. A few of the volumes may have contents lists. In terms of contents, there is no difference between these registers of deeds and those of other courts. You have to wade through many documents relating to debt to find the occasional marriage contract or will.

Local Courts Registers of Deeds

12.16 If you are looking for a deed dated earlier than 1748, then you might also look at the RH11 catalogue, to see if the records of a relevant 'local court' therein listed include a register of deeds. There is an index of courts by their place-name in the catalogue. The lists of court records note not only registers of deeds, but also the existence of deeds in other court books. For example, the regality of Kilwinning has a register of deeds for 1620-51 and 1664-96, part of the gap being filled with deeds entered in a court book. There are no indexes, but contents lists are noted when they occur.

12.17 Many deeds are scattered throughout the Gifts and Deposits and similar collections (see 6.19-20).

‿❧ *13* ❧‿

Litigants

13.1 Compiling registers of deeds was only a subsidiary part of the work of a court and the records of the main business of courts of law may contain information valuable to the ancestor-hunter. If your ancestor ran into debt or was of a disputatious nature and sufficiently prosperous, he probably got himself involved in litigation, and you will want to look for him in the records of those courts which dealt with legal disputes between private parties.

13.2 Your initial problem is – which court? There are courts that heard cases arising from any part of Scotland – the Court of Session, the Privy Council, the Admiralty Court, the Court of Exchequer. There were courts with a jurisdiction which was restricted to a particular administrative area – sheriff courts, commissary courts, burgh courts, Justice of the Peace courts, the 'franchise' courts. As most cases could be raised in more than one court and there were often appeals from a lower to a higher court, you may have to pursue your search in the records of several courts. It is difficult to give general advice on which court to start on. Maritime cases were heard by the Admiralty Court, cases involving marriage were heard by the Commissary Court of Edinburgh until 1830 (see 7.18-20), thereafter by the Court of Session; but apart from those, if the matter in dispute was minor, such as a small debt, you are best to start with a local court and, if the dispute was more significant, with the Court of Session.

Court of Session

13.3 Let us start with the highest civil court in Scotland, the Court of Session. It has a vast bulk of records, which are undersupplied with straightforward guides and are arranged in a complicated manner because that is the way the Court worked. Until 1821, the records of the Court were created within different offices, usually three concurrently. The cases were divided into two categories, those cases of which the final decree is 'extracted' and those of which it is not. If a decree was extracted, then it was copied into the Register of Acts and Decreets and the papers in the case preserved as 'extracted processes'. The records of all other cases, whether they reached decree or not, were preserved as 'unextracted processes'. There is no difference in legal validity between an extracted or an unextracted process. An extracted process is one which has completed its passage through the legal system i.e. one of the parties has had an extract of the court's determination made to enforce the court's decision. An unextracted process may have been abandoned at any previous stage. Even if the case reached a conclusion, the absence of an extract simply shows neither party felt the need to obtain an extract to enforce the court's judgement.

13.4 There is no distinction in content between extracted and unextracted cases or between the various offices. Consequently, you may have to examine several sets of records. To complicate matters further, at various times there have been divisions and separate departments of the Court of Session, with their own records. It is therefore difficult to explain simply how to gain access to the Court of Session records. However, we shall try, though you may still have to refer to the staff for further advice.

13.5 You had best start by looking at the guides to the Court of Session on the NAS website, or by reading the chapter on the Court of Session in *Guide to the National Archives of Scotland* (Stationery Office/Stair Society, 1996). These serve as an introduction to the Court's different functions, summarise the records briefly and are crucial in navigating your way around Court finding aids and records.

13.6 Your first task is to find out if there was a case before the Court of Session in which your ancestor was a party. Though there are some modern indexes, you will mostly have to look at the Court minute books and other imperfect guides. There are various problems. Often the cases will be described only by the surnames of the parties; indexes are usually of pursuers only, which is awkward if your ancestor was the defender; cases often change their names as they progress; cases often took several years to progress. Thus, Campbell v Macdonald, 1676, may later appear as Macdonald v Campbell, 1681. Though you may find short cuts, you will usually have to start by searching a minute book to ascertain if a case was heard by the Court, and persevere from there.

Court of Session before 1660

13.7 There are general minute books which note all the cases before the Court of Session, and particular minute books which note the cases dealt with by a particular office. Before 1650, the offices are called Scott, Gibson and Hay; between then and 1659, Brown and Durie. Because some of these minute books are damaged and therefore incomplete, you should check both general and particular ones. (If there is no surviving minute book, you can but read through the volumes of the Acts and Decreets.) The minute books are arranged chronologically and, under each date, list each legal action by the surnames of the opposing parties. The General Minute Books also supply the name of the relevant office, while the particular minute books will also tell you what happened to the action in the court on that day.

13.8 To illustrate, in a general minute book (CS8/3) at 3 July 1579 there is an entry 'act betx Hammiltoun qr Kynneir Gibson', which means that the Court that day heard an action between parties named Hamilton and Kinnear and that the case was recorded by Gibson's office. If you look in the Gibson particular minute book for that date (CS10/1) you will find 'Hamilton qr Kynneir – decernit' which confirms that there was a case between those parties on that date and that decree was granted. You then have to look at the CS catalogue for the Gibson volume of the Register of Acts and Decreets (CS7), which includes 3 July 1579 (CS7/76). As you do not have a folio reference, you look in the volume for the date (which is expressed in Latin) and the name of the parties in the margin; and you find a decree in favour of John Hammiltoun of Drumry against a tenant David Kynneir to remove from the lands of Craigfudies; which may or may not be what you want.

Court of Session 1661–1912

13.9 To find a case, first go to the general minute books. Until 1781, these are in manuscript (CS16). From 1782, they are printed (CS17). The manuscript ones are not indexed and you have to wade through the entries until you find one that seems relevant. The printed ones, which are annual, are indexed. These indexes are to all parties, distinguishing pursuers by the letter 'p' and defenders by the letter 'd', but give the surname only, except for some common surnames. The forenames, if given, may be in an abbreviated form, eg 'Ro' for 'Robert'. In the text of these minute books, there are further abbreviations for legal terms, such as 'P' for petition and 'D' for decree. The staff will advise you further on these.

13.10 In both manuscript and printed minute books, the entries are detailed and will therefore tell you if the case is one that will interest you or not. In the margin (manuscript) or as a heading (printed) there are some initials, eg 'H.J.L.', which are the clerk's mark, which you may need to trace the case further. Then there are some details about the case, the names and designations of the parties, and finally the names of the procurator (advocate) and judge. If you want more detail, you will then look elsewhere for the record of the case, which will usually be described by the pursuer's surname v the defender's surname.

13.11 First try the indexes to the Unextracted Processes. There are four card indexes divided chronologically, so look in the one that covers the date of the case (or two if the date is near the borderline). The first three of these are arranged by surname and chronologically within surname, while the fourth is arranged by surname and forename. These cards give an old reference, eg 2P.Y.5/3, which you will have to convert into the present call number. The first number and letter will always convert into a CS number, eg 2P becomes CS247. The rest of the old reference may still be used or may have to be converted into a running number: NAS staff will advise.

13.12 If you cannot find your case in these card indexes, next try what is called the Carmichael and Elliot arrangement of processes (CS98–CS227). These are fully searchable through the electronic catalogue.

13.13 Still no success? You now want to try the Register of Acts and Decreets. How to search this depends on the date you are searching.

13.14 Up to 1810 look again at the clerk's mark which you found in the minute book. Refer to a guide to clerks' marks which will tell you whether this particular clerk was employed in the DAL, DUR or MACK offices. You now want to look at the relevant extractor's minute book. Of these, DAL is now CS19; DUR is CS23; and MACK is CS27. An entry gives simply the date and surnames of the parties. If you find a relevant entry, order out the equivalent volume of the Register of Acts and Decreets, which was kept in the three offices, again DAL (CS18), DUR (CS22), and MACK (CS26). If you want to see the warrants or papers in the case (known as 'extracted processes'), you order by CS21 (DAL), CS25 (DUR) or CS29 (MACK) plus the date and the names of the parties. These processes may not add anything to what you find in the Register, in which written pleadings are given at great length. A seventeenth-century judge described the bulk of decreets as 'nauseous'!

[2]   *July* 27. 1761.

MEMORIAL

FOR

Poor PETER WILLIAMSON late of the Province of *Penſylvania* in *North America*, Planter, now Reſidenter in *Edinburgh*: Purſuer,

AGAINST

Alexander Cuſhnie late Dean-of-Guild and Procurator-Fiſcal of the Borough-Court of *Aberdeen*, and others: Defenders.

With an Abſtract of the Proof.

THE Purſuer was born in the pariſh of Hirnley in Aberdeenſhire, in the month of February 1730, and continued with his father, who was a reputable tenant in that country, till about the year 1740, when he was ſent to ſchool at Aberdeen, where he lived under the care and inſpection of an Aunt. At that time it was a common practice among the merchants in Aberdeen to pick up young boys from the ſtreet and in the country, whom they confined in barns and other convenient places, till ſuch time as they had got together a ſufficient number of them, when they uſed to ſend them to America, and there ſold them as ſlaves. It was the misfortune of the Purſuer to fall into the hands of one employed by Bailie William Fordyce and Company merchants in Aberdeen, to pick up

A   boys

Printed memorial setting out the case of Peter Williamson (CS29/103/1/1762).

13.15 From 1810 onwards there are annual indexes to the Register of Acts and Decreets. Within each year and within each initial letter of surname, the order is chronological. The entry tells you the type of case, the names (usually just surnames) of the parties and the date the decree was extracted. You then have to find the relevant CS number and the volume number of that CS series which includes that date. The equivalent extracted process is ordered out by the relevant CS number, date and names of parties. These processes may include information not in the Register.

13.16 Let us now look at some examples.

13.17 In a General Minute Book (CS16/1/54) under the date 11th February 1721 you find an entry 'Decreet in absence Elizabeth and Helen Monteiths Daughters to umqull Alexander Monteith of Todshaugh chirurgeon in Edinburgh and their husbands contra John Fultoun chirurgeon in Douglas'. You do not find this case in the Unextracted Processes or Carmichael and Elliot indexes, but in the DAL Extractors Minute Book for that date (CS19/1/3) you find 'D [= decree] Monteiths q Fulton'. Therefore you order out the volume of the Register of Acts and Decreets, series DAL, for that date (CS18/204) and look through it to find the full report of the case, which supplies the names of the ladies' husbands and shows that the case was brought to retrieve debts owed to the deceased Alexander Monteith for 'drugs and medicaments furnished by him'. You may also order out the extracted process relevant to the case, which is CS21/1721 February 11/Monteiths v Fulton.

13.18 In a General Minute Book (CS16/1/132) under the date 27th January 1768 you find a case brought by Christian Allan, daughter to James Allan, late bailie of Hamilton, against John McNeill, schoolmaster in Hamilton. You look up the Unextracted Process card index and find 'Allan, Christian v McNiel 1767 Adams Mack A1/101'. This number converts into CS229/A1/101 which you order out and find that the action was for non-payment of rent of a house owned by the pursuer in the Castlewynd of Hamilton. (You may then try the Register of Sasines in the hope of finding more information.)

13.19 Having looked up the name 'Lindsay' in the index to the 1815-16 printed general minute book (CS17/1/35) you find a case heard by the First Division of the Court on 28 February 1816 'D [ecree] in ab [sence] David Freer, WS. AG [ainst] Sam [uel] Lindsay, brewer in Dunkeld'.

109

The clerk's mark is M.H.B. You then look in the Acts and Decreets index for 1816 and find the entry 'Freer v Lindsay' with the date of extract 16 July 1816. 'M.H.B.' is the mark for volumes of the Register of Acts and Decreets referenced CS39 and extracted processes referenced CS40. You order out CS39/22 and look through this volume until you find the decree. The case is a simple one of debt.

13.20 Divorce cases were the responsibility of the Court of Session after 1830 and to find them up to 1912 you look initially at the printed minute books. You are looking for the divorce case of a couple named McKay. The index in the minute book for 1884 (CS17/1/103) leads you to an entry under the date 22nd January 1884, describing a decree of divorce in favour of Janet Rankin, or Lean, or Mckay, residing in Creetown, against James McKay, residing at Xenia, in the State of Ohio, in the United States of America. The minute also names their daughter, and his sister and mother, who live in Newton Stewart. As you want more information, you look up the index to Unextracted Processes and find a card 'McKay, Janet Rankin or Lean or, v Mckay, Divorce 1882, 2P.Mc.14/2' which number converts into CS247/4184. You order out this process and discover that the defender went to America to gain employment but has not been heard of for several years.

Court of Session since 1913

13.21 After 1912, there are annual indexes to the Unextracted Processes, and you may prefer to go straight to this index and then to the index to the Acts and Decreets, though the General Minute Books are still the best guide to which cases were heard by the Court of Session. The minute books end in 1990. Indexes to Unextracted Processes, 1913-1994, and to Acts and Decreets, 1952-1994, are searchable through the electronic catalogue. The annual indexes to Unextracted Processes are, as usual, indexes to pursuers only, giving also the nature of the process, the name of the defender and the year the case was called, which will be earlier than the year of the index.

13.22 In 1995, separate indexes of Unextracted and Extracted Processes were discontinued by the Court, and a single combined index has been produced since then. The Court also adopted a simplified divorce procedure from 1983, which forms a separate series. Both series of records are searchable through the electronic catalogue.

Bill Chamber

13.23 You may have come across cases in the minute books which you have not been able to trace or you simply wish to search further among the Court of Session records. There are some guides which we have not yet consulted. Most notably there are indexes to the Bill Chamber processes (CS271), the Bill Chamber being a court within the Court of Session. The CS catalogue explains its functions. The index (of pursuers) covers the years 1670-1852 and is searchable on the electronic catalogue.

Jury Court

13.24 The Jury Court existed between 1815 and 1850 to hear cases referred to a jury by the Court of Session. A searchable index is available on the electronic catalogue.

Accountant of Court

13.25 The office of Accountant of Court (records from 1739) has responsibility in the supervision of estates of children and other persons unable to administer their own affairs. If you are seeking actions concerning the guardianship of infants or the appointment of factors loco tutoris, you should examine these records (CS313-317). You will remember that a tutor is appointed to administer the affairs of a fatherless child (see 9.5 onwards). If you fail to find a record of the appointment of a tutor in the record of Retours, you should try the records of the Accountant of Court. There are indexes available and CS313-314 and CS316-317 are searchable through the electronic catalogue. You may find sufficient detail in the printed minute book, however.

Sequestrations

13.26 Over the years, a sadly large number of Scots have become bankrupt and methods have had to be found to satisfy their creditors. The earlier main legal method, cessio bonorum, was largely superseded by sequestration which dates from 1771. Since then, there have been regular reforms, attempting to provide justice for all parties concerned. These regular changes in the system mean that there is a variety of paths to follow to find a particular sequestration case. In some cases, the bankrupt will be the pursuer; in some cases, a creditor.

Bankrupts before 1839

13.27 Before 1839, to look for a bankruptcy case among the Court of Session records, you can use the procedures described above for all cases. From August 1783, you have the alternative of looking first in the printed index to the General Register of Inhibitions (see 13.58-60), as from that date all petitions for sequestration had to be recorded in that register. It is the bankrupt who is indexed and therefore you will find out if it is worth searching the Court of Session records for the case. An additional path is to look at the published and indexed *List of Court of Session Productions* (List and Index Society), which lists most of the business books (CS96) found in Court of Session processes. These books include sederunt books compiled by the trustees in bankruptcy and the entries in the *List* provide the reference of the sequestration process to which the sederunt book refers. The CS96 index is searchable through the electronic catalogue.

Bankrupts since 1839

13.28 For this period, you have to check three series of processes, CS280, CS318 (which is the current record series) and CS319. These are searchable on the electronic catalogue, as are some other minor record sequestration series such as petitions and appeals. You may wish to consult 'A Guide to Scottish Sequestrations, 1839-1913', available in the search room, which provides an introduction to sequestration finding aids and records.

13.29 Sheriff courts also dealt with bankruptcy cases. Look at the contents list of the records of the relevant sheriff court (SC) for 'Register of Sequestrations'. There is a useful guide to these in the Court of Session records, as after 1840 sheriff clerks made returns to the Court of Session of sequestrations depending before their court (CS283, 331 and 332).

Privy Council

13.30 The Court of Session was, in origin, an offshoot of the Privy Council, which had judicial as well as administrative functions. The Privy Council continued to act in a judicial capacity up to 1707, issuing decrees, or making an effort 'to agree the parties', or referring a case to the Court of Session or a lower court. It tended to be the better-off complainant who took a case to the Privy Council.

13.31 The *Register of the Privy Council of Scotland* is published up to 1691, each volume being fully indexed. If you are looking for a case between 1545 and 1691, look up the name of the party in the index of the printed volume for the relevant period. The printed text is quite full, but if you want to see the original, order by PC1, up to August 1610, or PC2, after that date, and the volume number given in the PC catalogue for the date of that entry.

13.32 Between 1692 and 1695, you have no choice but to look in the original volumes of the Registers of Decreta (PC2/24-26): look for the brief description of each entry in the margin. Between 1696 and 1707, look in the minute books (PC4/2-3) which describe all the business of the Council, not just the judicial business. There you will find such entries as 'Lybell Bruce of Pitterthie agt Corstorphine of Neydie Called and remitted to the Judge ordinar' (26 January 1697), which will show if it is worthwhile examining the PC2 volumes.

Admiralty Court

13.33 The Admiralty Court had jurisdiction in all maritime and seafaring cases, both civil and criminal, until 1830, when its civil jurisdiction was transferred to the Court of Session. If your ancestor was a shipowner or shipmaster or merchant who traded overseas, then he may have been involved in an action before the Admiralty Court.

13.34 Look at the Admiralty Court catalogue (AC). The records that concern you are the decreets and processes (AC7, 8, 9, 10, 15), to which there are guides in the form of roughly chronological lists of cases. Argyll and the Isles were the responsibility of a separate Vice-Admiralty Court, whose jurisdiction ran from Dumbarton Castle to Cape Wrath. A modern index to matters brought before it, 1685-1825, has been compiled by Mr W Bigwood, Flat B, The Lodge, 2 East Road, North Berwick, EH39 4HN, from whom copies may be purchased; the index may also be consulted in the West Search Room.

13.35 AC7 consists of volumes of decreets, 1627-1830. To obtain the guide to them, order out AC7/107. This lists the surnames of pursuer and defender, the date and the volume number; eg 'Mitchell Mackenzie 2 July 1725 Vol. 30'. To see that decreet, you order out AC7/30. If you are lucky, the volume will have a contents list, giving the folio number on which the decreet starts.

13.36 AC8, 9, 10 and 15, which date from or after 1702, each have a modern contents list available in the Search Room. These give the decree or process number, the names of the pursuer and defender and the year; eg, 'AC10/563 Brymer, Magnus v James Hutton 1779'. This is a case brought by an apprentice sailmaker in Leith who joined the navy and was then incarcerated at the instance of his master until he found someone to guarantee the completion of his apprenticeship. The majority of cases are less interesting, being mainly for payment.

Court of Exchequer

13.37 Between 1708 and 1856 (when its jurisdiction was transferred to the Court of Session), the Court of Exchequer dealt with revenue cases, including debts to the Crown, seizure of smuggled goods and prosecutions for illicit brewing and distilling. Unfortunately, its records generally provide little information about individuals and there are no indexes. To investigate, look first at the minute books (E351), which will give the names but not the designations of the parties in the cases. If you find a case which seems relevant, look further at the books of orders (E352), the enrolled or original informations, which may provide designations but which are in various rather abstruse series (see the catalogue – E358-368), and the affidavits, which can be informative but many have not survived (E376). If your ancestor owed money to the Crown between 1711 and 1827, there may be an inventory of his property in a series referenced E371.

Sheriff Courts

13.38 Apart from the Court of Session, the court in which your ancestor would most likely be a litigant would be a sheriff court. There are the following sheriff courts, each with jurisdiction over all or part of a county. Each has its own catalogue.

County	Sheriff Courts
Aberdeen	Aberdeen (SC1); Peterhead (SC4)
Angus (Forfar)	Arbroath (SC43); Dundee (SC45); Forfar (SC47)
Argyll	Campbeltown (SC50); Dunoon (SC51); Fort William (SC52); Inverary (SC54); Oban (SC57); Tobermory (SC59)
Ayr	Ayr (SC6); Kilmarnock (SC7)
Banff	Banff (SC2)

County	Sheriff Courts
Berwick	Duns (SC60)
Bute	Rothesay (SC8)
Caithness	Wick (SC14)
Clackmannan	Alloa (SC64)
Dumfries	Dumfries (SC15)
Dunbarton	Dumbarton (SC65)
East Lothian (Haddington)	Haddington (SC40)
Edinburgh City	Edinburgh (SC39); Leith (SC69)
Fife	Cupar (SC20); Dunfermline (SC21); Kirkcaldy (SC23)
Glasgow	Glasgow (SC36)
Inverness	Fort William (SC28); Inverness (SC29); Lochmaddy (SC30); Portree (SC32)
Kincardine	Stonehaven (SC5)
Kinross	Kinross (SC22)
Kirkcudbright	Kirkcudbright (SC16); Dumfries (SC17)
Lanark	Airdrie (SC35); Glasgow (SC36); Hamilton (SC37); Lanark (SC38)
Midlothian (Edinburgh)	Edinburgh (SC39)
Moray (Elgin)	Elgin (SC26)
Nairn	Nairn (SC31)
Orkney	Kirkwall (SC11 – in Kirkwall); Orkney and Shetland (SC10 – 17th century only)
Peebles	Peebles (SC42)
Perth	Dunblane (SC44); Perth (SC49)
Renfrew	Greenock (SC53); Paisley (SC58)
Ross and Cromarty	Cromarty (SC24); Dingwall (SC25); Stornoway (SC33); Tain (SC34)
Roxburgh	Jedburgh (SC62)
Selkirk	Selkirk (SC63)
Shetland	Lerwick (SC12 – in Lerwick); Orkney and Shetland (SC10 – 17th century only)
Stirling	Falkirk (SC66); Stirling (SC67)
Sutherland	Dornoch (SC9)
West Lothian (Linlithgow)	Linlithgow (SC41)
Wigtown	Stranraer (SC18); Wigtown (SC19)

13.39 First, decide which sheriff court(s) had jurisdiction where your ancestor was, and then look at the relevant sheriff court catalogue. In its contents list, look at the records of the 'Ordinary Court', which are usually at the start of the catalogue.

13.40 There is little consistency among the various sheriff courts in the names they gave their series of records or in the contents thereof. Even within one series, there may be considerable variety in the sort of detail provided. There is tremendous variation in the starting date of surviving records and there may be unexplained gaps. Indexes to sheriff court cases for Midlothian decrees (SC39/8) 1830–1900 and to Perthshire processes (SC44/22) 1809–1900, are available.

13.41 Depending on what categories of records have been created by each sheriff court and on what has survived, to search for a case you may have to look at minute books, act books, diet books or court books, around the appropriate date, or, from the late nineteenth century, registers of ordinary actions and of summary applications. It will be up to you to decide how to proceed. There will often also be a register of decrees and one or more series of processes.

13.42 For instance, if you are looking for a case in the Sheriff Court of Hamilton after 1770, you should look first at the minute books (SC37/4) to find the case, then at the act books (SC37/2) for details of the case, and, if the case reached decree, at the decree books (SC37/7) for more detail. You may also want to search for the process (SC37/8).

13.43 The sort of cases you may be seeking in the sheriff court records are actions for aliment, affiliation orders, registration of irregular marriages, small debt, workmen's compensation. Sometimes these cases will be found mixed among all the other cases, sometimes they will be in a separate volume or series. For example, the Aberdeen sheriff court has a separate alimentary register 1903–24 (SC1/7/19) in the midst of the records of decrees.

13.44 Actions for registration of irregular marriages date after 1859 and are unlikely to provide information additional to that to be found in the official registers of marriages. Civil processes after 1860 are not retained in their entirety and many which were not considered worth preserving have been destroyed. There is a rolling programme to catalogue the surviving processes and many are now searchable on the electronic catalogue.

Valentine from a Sheriff Court process, produced as evidence in an action for breach of promise (SC58/22/630)

The names of the parties, nature of the action and date are recorded in full.

13.45 In a sheriff court catalogue, the records of workmen's compensation cases, that is, for compensation for personal injury by accident in course of employment, are usually placed separately from those of the ordinary court. They date from 1898.

Commissary Courts

13.46 As well as dealing with executry matters, the commissary courts had a civil jurisdiction until 1823. Most of the actions heard by the courts other than the Edinburgh Commissary Court (7.18-20) were for debt.

13.47 Look at the table at 8.7 which shows which commissary court had jurisdiction within which modern counties. Then look in the CC catalogue for the list of records of the relevant commissariot. The records of civil actions are called act or diet books, minute books and registers of decrees, and processes. There are no indexes. All the cases should be noted in the Act or Diet Books, but often the record is brief and will probably not say what the action was about. The Registers of Decrees give a full report of the cases, but not all the cases reached decrees.

Justice of the Peace Courts

13.48 A civil case could be brought before the Justices of the Peace of the relevant county, but, apart from small debt cases (since 1795), the records of this civil jurisdiction are rather sparse, which is a pity as the JP courts sometimes heard cases of aliment.

13.49 If you want to search this record, look at the contents list of the JP catalogue for the relevant county or city and then at the court books in the records of that JP court. The records of some of these courts have been transferred to local archives.

Burgh Courts

13.50 If your ancestor resided in a royal burgh, he might have been a litigant in the burgh court. Look at the list of records of the particular burgh in the B catalogue, to see if these include court books or a register of decreets. The NAS does not hold such records for the majority of burghs, but they may be held by a local archive. These court books can vary tremendously in content, from simply stating the name of the parties to full copies of the decreets. The vast majority of the cases heard in the burgh courts were for debt. There are no indexes.

Franchise Courts

13.51 The Crown used to franchise local justice to certain landowners, who could hold courts in their own lands and administer justice over their vassals and tenants. There were four types of these courts – regality, barony, stewartry and bailiary. Most were abolished in 1747 and the rest thereafter quickly declined into insignificance.

13.52 Look at the RH11 catalogue. This has an index of courts, which directs you to the local court records in the RH11 series and also those in other classes of records. If you find a required place-name in the index and then go to the list of records of that local court, the records of litigation you require will be usually described as 'court books' or 'minutes of court'. The reports of cases in these are generally rather summary, sometimes just giving the names of the parties, but you may be lucky. The commonest actions before such courts are for payment and between landlord and tenant.

13.53 These court books are not indexed and are compiled in a variety of handwritings which make them particularly difficult to decipher. However, a few of them have been published, such as those of the regality of Melrose (Scottish History Society).

Diligence

13.54 Your ancestor's name may also appear in the records of the procedures whereby the courts tried to enforce their decrees. For this purpose, a document registered for execution in a register of deeds (see 12.2) counts as a decree. The generic term for these procedures is diligence. The individual documents are known as 'letters of' that particular form of diligence. The commonest are letters of horning. You may be seeking such letters because you have come across a reference to them in a document or case record, or because you suspect that they may have followed on a registered deed or court decision, or just in a general trawl for your ancestors. They largely relate to debt situations.

13.55 Of the various forms of diligence, there are three main forms of which registers were kept and therefore provide consistent records in a consultative form. These are registers of hornings, inhibitions and apprisings or adjudications. There were general registers for each, covering the whole of Scotland, and particular registers of hornings and inhibitions kept within counties and regalities. After 1781, there are indexes to the registers of inhibitions and adjudications. Otherwise, you have to search the minute books or, if there are no minute books, the record itself. Look at the Diligence (DI) catalogue to see what volumes and minute books are available.

Hornings

13.56 Letters of horning charged a debtor to pay or perform as the court instructed. They were much used and affected most classes of society. If the debtor failed to obey the letters of horning, they could be registered, opening the way for sterner measures, including imprisonment and forfeiture of goods. Registration might be either in the general register of hornings or the particular register for the county or (until 1748) regality where the parties were. As there are no indexes, you have to know the approximate date and place for your search.

13.57 However, the minute books are clear and informative about the parties, who are expressed in the creditor against the debtor format, eg in the general minute book on 1st of April 1701 (expressed in Latin) we find an entry 'Mary Haigs Eldest Laull daughter of James Haigs Gairdner at Dalkeith Agt John Mair Portioner of Pinky commonly called Greinwalls' (DI2/17). This turns out to be an untypical case, because when we get out the volume of the register for that date (DI1/345) we find that Mair is being sued for a penalty for not fulfilling a contract to marry Mary Haigs.

Inhibitions

13.58 Inhibitions were designed (a) to prevent a debtor from disposing of his heritable property to the detriment of his creditor; and (b) to stop a husband's liability for his wife's debts. From 1783, petitions for sequestration were also recorded in the general register of inhibitions. Thus, this record is only worth investigating if your ancestor was likely to have owned land or a house, or had a broken marriage, or went bankrupt. The property is not named. Again you may have to investigate three registers – the general register of inhibitions, and the particular registers for the county (until 1869) or regality (until 1748). After 1869, there is only the general register. To search these up to 1780, you have to use the minute books, which are clear and detailed. From 1781, there are indexes, separate ones for the general register (printed up to 1868, then manuscript) and for the particular registers for each county (printed).

13.59 These are indexes of the parties inhibited or sequestrated, i.e. the debtor or the wife or the bankrupt. The indexes give the name and designation of the person inhibited or sequestrated, the name of the inhibiter (plus designation if a husband), the date, the volume number (in roman numerals) and the folio number (in arabic numerals). Within each surname, companies are indexed before individuals. Women are indexed by their maiden name. Sequestrations are distinguished by the abbreviation '*Seq.*' instead of '*Inhib*'.

13.60 You order out by the DI series number, which you obtain from the catalogue, and the volume number (converted into arabic). For example, in the index to the general register of inhibitions, you find 'DICKIE, John, merchant, Dunfermline. *Seq.* Mar. 19. 1788. – cciv.931' and therefore you order out DI8/204 and look up folio 931: or in the index to the particular register for Haddington you find 'BEGBIE, Marion; *Inhib.* by James Telfer, Labourer, Haddington, her husband, Jan. 30. 1811-xxii.422.' and order out DI60/22 and look up folio 422.

Apprisings and Adjudications

13.61 If a creditor wished to attach and obtain ownership of the heritable property of a debtor in satisfaction for a debt, then he had to obtain a decree of apprising (until 1672) or adjudication (from 1672) against the debtor. From 1636, these decrees were copied into a register (DI13 and 14), the adjudications in a sensibly abbreviated form. Although these were decrees of the Court of Session, it is easier to trace apprisings and adjudications in these registers than in the records of the Court.

13.62 Until 1780, they have to be searched by means of the minute books, which are mostly nicely detailed; with the surname of the main debtor in the margin. The volume number and call number is found in the DI catalogue. From 1781, there are indexes, printed up to 1868, thereafter manuscript. These index the debtor, supplying the names and designations of both debtor and creditor, the date, and volume and folio numbers: eg 'WEIR, Andrew, late candlemaker, Edinburgh, now abroad, and Janet Kettle, his spouse; *By* Janet Swanston, in East Register Street, Edinburgh, Apr.23.1818.-clxvi.74.' The catalogue provides the reference DI14/166. The adjudication starting on folio 74 therein does not, alas, tell us why Andrew is abroad, but does give a detailed description of the lodging house adjudged from the Weirs.

13.63 These decrees and their abbreviates specify the lands to be apprised or adjudged. Obviously, you will only want to inspect this register if your ancestor owned heritable property. It is quite useful to genealogists because of the practice of pursuing the heirs of deceased debtors. In these cases, the relationship of the heir or heirs to the deceased debtor will be explained. For example, in the minute book for 21st August 1754 (DI15/15), you will find an entry labelled 'Macquaintances', which lists three members of that uncommon family who are pursued as heirs of an uncle and cousin named Forbes. The register (DI14/97) supplies no further genealogical information to that which is in the minute book.

Imprisonment

13.64 Until 1880, it was quite common for debtors who could not pay to be imprisoned at the instance of their creditors. Thus, their names may appear in prison registers along with people accused of and found guilty of crimes (see Chapter 14).

Sanctuary

13.65 Until 1880, civil debtors might avoid diligence by taking sanctuary in the palace of Holyroodhouse. There is a copy of the register of those who took this step at RH2/8/17–20. It is not indexed.

$\mathcal{G}14\mathcal{G}$

Criminals

14.1 It is an irony of ancestor-hunting that you are more likely to find information about an ancestor who committed a crime than one who was a respectable, law-abiding citizen. Such information may be found in records of the inquiries into the case, records of various criminal courts, and in prison records. Most of the records detailed in this chapter are available in the West Search Room of the NAS at West Register House.

14.2 The NAS is creating electronic catalogue entries to improve access to criminal trial records, particularly the more serious offences heard before the High Court of Justiciary, the supreme criminal court in Scotland, and to Crown Office precognitions. Trials in the High Court were held before a judge and jury, and are known as 'solemn' trials, as opposed to those held before a judge alone, known as 'summary' trials. In the High Court catalogue you will find the person's full name, crimes accused, where and when tried, outcome and final sentencing. In the Precognitions catalogue you may find additional personal details such as age, designation, occupation and address. Some catalogue entries also contain details about the victims of crime (though only after 100 years) and where the crime took place. The catalogue will also provide the references of related papers; for example if a precognition resulted in a trial, you will find the reference of the relevant trial papers in the catalogue entry for the precognition.

Precognitions

14.3 A precognition is the written report of the evidence of witnesses to a crime, taken before the trial to help prepare the case against the accused (whether or not he ever comes to trial). Precognitions for the more serious crimes are preserved among the Lord Advocate's or Crown Office records (AD). Hardly any survive before 1812. Up to 1900, the precognitions are referenced AD14, and, from 1901, AD15. The second number in each reference represents the year, e.g. an 1834 precognition

Wanted poster, 1909. From the Lord Advocate's Department records (AD15/9/166).

will be numbered AD14/34. There is a 75-year closure period for precognitions. Those that are open are catalogued by year, by the name of the accused. Where the information occurs in the record the catalogue will also mention their full designation, occupation, age and address. Here you will find records of labourers, servants, hawkers and others who leave little or no trace in property records.

14.4 If you believe that your ancestor was suspected of committing a crime during the nineteenth or early twentieth centuries, search the NAS electronic catalogue using the name of the accused. You will find such entries as AD14/34/373 'James Robertson, alias David Smith, alias James Burns, Cotton Spinner, Calton, Glasgow, Native of Manchester, aged 26'. He was indicted, or charged, with 'Theft by housebreaking and previous conviction'. His co-accused was 'James McMehen, alias McMicham, Painter, Main Street, Gorbals, Glasgow', charged as an accomplice with 'Theft by housebreaking'. Precognitions contain not only statements by the witnesses, but also a declaration by the accused. If you order out James Robertson's precognition, you will find that he declared that he had committed a theft in 1826, and been sentenced to transportation for seven years, and had returned to Glasgow in 1833. For this second offence, Robertson was sentenced to transportation for life by the High Court in Edinburgh on 14 July 1834, while McMehan was found not guilty and dismissed from the court (JC8/32, f. 89r). Crimes which led to a sentence of transportation are likely to be found among the Precognitions.

14.5 Two other of the Lord Advocate's records provide useful reports of the progress of such criminal investigations. (They too are closed for 75 years.) From 1822, there are procedure books (AD9), which are arranged, first by geographical areas, and then chronologically. They record the name (not designation) of the accused, the crime and whether the case was to be brought to trial or not, and by what court. You will then know what court record to search for the details of the trial. Even more useful, but unfortunately dating only from 1890, is AD8, a series of ledgers which record all criminal cases reported to the Crown Agent, giving the name (not designation) of the accused, details of the crime, date and place of the trial, the plea, verdict and sentence. The arrangement is by first letter of the accused's surname and then chronological.

High Court of Justiciary

14.6 Apart from the Precognitions after 1812, the principal source to search for information about a criminal ancestor is the records of the High Court of Justiciary, the supreme criminal court in Scotland. Its records, most of which are open to public inspection, are listed in the electronic JC catalogue. The Court sat both in Edinburgh and on circuit in other parts of Scotland. If a crime was committed in the Edinburgh area, the case would usually be tried in Edinburgh. Otherwise, it might be tried either in Edinburgh or on circuit.

14.7 The records of the Edinburgh sittings are contained in the Books of Adjournal (JC2-5) and minute books (JC6-9). Both of these report the trials fully. All trials for the nineteenth and twentieth centuries have been indexed on the electronic catalogue, and references for any trial record over

75 years old can be found on the online version. For trials which took place fewer than 75 years ago, you will only be able to consult the catalogue in the NAS search rooms.

14.8 For earlier centuries, indexing is ongoing and indexes and catalogues will become available as they are completed. There are older indexes for the periods 1611-1631 and 1699-1720. Selected trials have been published in Robert Pitcairn's *Criminal Trials in Scotland, 1498-1624* (3 volumes, Bannatyne Club), *Selected Justiciary Cases, 1624-50* (3 volumes, Stair Society, ed. Stair Gillon) and *Records of the Proceedings of the Justiciary Court, Edinburgh, 1661-1678*, ed. W Scott-Moncrieff (2 volumes, Scottish History Society).

14.9 For trials not yet indexed, or on the electronic catalogue, you should look for the name of an accused in bound copies of manuscript lists of cases heard by the High Court in Edinburgh. These lists are inaccurately entitled as indexes, but were effectively 'diet books' or procedure books of the court. The accused is usually described as the 'Pannel', and may be noted only on his first appearance, though the trial may continue over several days. If there are several accused in one trial, only one may be named in the list. If you find the name of an accused who interests you, look at the Books of Adjournal and/or minute books for the date given. For example, we find on 5 January 1736, the pannel is 'Barrisdale' and the crime is 'subborning witnesses'. This, incidentally, illustrates one problem of these indexes in that 'Barrisdale' is not a surname but a territorial designation; lairds in Scotland were usually known by the names of their estates. The owner in this case was Coll McDonell, younger of Barrisdale. We find the record his trial in JC3/20 and JC7/20; it continued until 10 February, when he was acquitted.

14.10 If you suspect that your ancestor was accused of a crime and he does not appear in the High Court in Edinburgh, then it is possible that he was tried by the Court on circuit. The areas where the Court sat on circuit during the nineteenth century were Aberdeen, Inverness and Perth (the North circuit); Ayr, Dumfries and Jedburgh (the South circuit) and Glasgow, Inveraray and Stirling (the West circuit). The records of the Court on circuit are minute books (JC10-14), which exist from 1655 and fully report the trials. From 1890, there are also Circuit Books of Adjournal (JC15). To find a case during the nineteenth and early twentieth centuries, as with cases before the High Court, Edinburgh, search the electronic catalogue under the name of the accused. Further information about circuit cases between 1830 and 1887 can be found in the AD6 volumes which list all circuit cases for that period, giving the name of the accused plus the verdict and sentence. If you find the name you seek, you can then study the account of the trial in the JC circuit minute book. From 1887 there are lists available in the West Search Room of cases for each circuit court. Another record you may consult is the Circuit Books of Appeal (JC22) which date from 1748 and record appeals from lower courts to the circuit courts. These contain no index and you must just read through the record.

14.11 An alternative source of information about nineteenth and twentieth century Justiciary Court cases may be found in the Lord Advocate's records. AD2-5 consist of bound copies of printed indictments, which give full details of each accused and crime, and list the witnesses for each trial. AD2 has High Court indictments, 1829-91, and AD3 circuit court indictments, 1839-87, each volume including a contents list of names of accused. AD4 contains indictments relating to postal offences, 1822-74. AD5 contains miscellaneous High and circuit court indictments, 1837-43, with no contents list, but annotated with each verdict and sentence. Details from some of these entries have been added to the Justiciary trials electronic catalogue.

14.12 If your ancestor was transported as punishment for committing a crime, then the record of his trial should be in the JC records. Transportation ceased to be used as a punishment in 1857, but some prisoners sentenced to penal servitude were transported until 1867 (see 14.23).

Privy Council

14.13 Until 1707, criminal cases might also be dealt with by the Privy Council. To find such a case, follow the advice in 13.30-32.

Sheriff Courts

14.14 If your criminal ancestor was not tried in the High Court, the next most likely court to have judged him is the sheriff court (see list at 13.38). The commonest crimes to be tried there were theft and assault. Assuming that you know where your ancestor was in Scotland, look in the contents list of the catalogue of the records of the relevant sheriffdom(s) for the Criminal Court records. The criminal records of the various sheriff courts bear various titles and start at widely varying dates. The main record, reporting the trials, may be called 'Criminal Court Books', 'Criminal Record', 'Criminal Register', 'Record of Criminal Trials', etc. The only indexes are within some of the volumes of the record themselves. These supply only surname and forename and only at the first appearance. In some sheriff courts, there are separate records of trials heard by the sheriff with a jury (solemn trials) and those heard by the sheriff sitting alone (summary trials). If there are no criminal court records for the years you are searching, try the ordinary court records, which sometimes report both civil and criminal cases. Check also in the catalogue for criminal libels and/or indictments, as these sometimes survive from an earlier date than the court record. These may include various relative papers, such as a declaration by the accused. For instance, in 1828, the sheriff court of Lanark investigated a charge against one John Anderson for passing forged bank notes. His declaration shows that he was a pedlar, about 19 years of age, usually residing in Castle Douglas, born in Girvan, where his father resided, and was bred a weaver (SC38/55/1).

14.15 Minor offences were usually tried in local courts. Until 1747, such offenders might be brought before one of the 'franchise' courts, which are described in 13.51-53. As criminal courts, they heard such cases as assault ('blood and ryot') and scandal and illegal fishing. Occasionally, such a court dealt with a serious offence, eg in 1666 James Cramond was banished from the town of Kelso for theft (RH11/42/1). In the administration of such courts, there was no practical distinction made between civil and criminal cases, which are intermingled in the court books.

14.16 A unique franchise court was the Argyll Justiciary Court which had criminal jurisdiction throughout Argyll and the Western Isles. Its records, which date from 1664 to 1742, have been published in the *Argyll Justiciary Records* (Stair Society) in two volumes, which are indexed. The reference numbers of the originals of the original records are now SC54/17/1/1-4.

Burgh Courts

14.17 Minor offences within royal burghs would be tried by the burgh court. Again, the records of such trials are intermingled in the court books with the other business of the court (see 13.50). Most offences tried by a burgh court were of the nature of a breach of a peace, but their records have a particular genealogical value in that these courts fined the participants in irregular marriages. For example, in Peebles in 1728, James Montgomery, cripple, for the present residing in Peebles, and Jean Drysdale were fined by the magistrates for their irregular marriage by the vicar of Irthington (in Cumberland) on 8th March 1726. Jean Drysdale was later banished from the burgh for another offence (B58/9/4).

Justice of the Peace Courts

14.18 See 13.48-49 for how to search the JP records. The JP courts also had a criminal jurisdiction. The records in the court books are usually brief and the offences charged vary from court to court. In country areas, the commonest crime was pursuit of game (i.e. poaching). In towns, the offences were more varied – theft, scandal, riot, breach of peace, being a whore. Occasionally, people were fined for irregular marriage or witnessing one. For example, in 1728, Antony Aston, comedian in Edinburgh, was fined for being witness to his son Walter's irregular marriage with Mrs Jean Kerr (JP35/4/2).

Admiralty Court

14.19 If your ancestor committed a crime on the high seas up to 1830, then the record of his trial may be among the Admiralty Court records. In the AC catalogue, look up AC16, which lists the volumes that contain the reports of these trials. They date from 1705. There is no index, but each volume has a contents list. There are also separate indexes to processes by the surnames of the parties. Very few cases were in fact heard by the Admiralty Court.

Witnesses

14.20 The electronic catalogue has opened up new possibilities for research. Previously, it is unlikely anyone would have thought of looking for an ancestor who was a witness or a juror in a trial. However, this invaluable resource is now bringing to light individuals who were previously difficult to trace. Details of some witnesses, jurors and also victims of crime are available through the catalogue. The depositions of witnesses are a valuable genealogical source among records of criminal trials, formerly inaccessible because any indexing or listing was done by name of the accused. Yet when a witness gave evidence, his age, marital status, trade and place of abode were all recorded. Such depositions are found most commonly in the Precognitions and the High Court of Justiciary records. Here are two examples: from a precognition, 1834 – 'John McDonald, aged fourteen, son of, and residing with Dougal McDonald, porter at the

Broomilaw, Glasgow' (AD14/34/373); from a trial record, 1736 – 'Evan More McAphie alias Cameron formerly in Shian in Glengarry parish of Kilinanivage and shire of Inverness now in Kilin in the shire of Perth aged 52 years or thereby married' (JC7/2O).

Jurors

14.21 Like witnesses, the appearance of jurors at the 'assize' are another genea-logical source among the records of criminal trials. In most cases they remain unknown, again because listing or indexing is done by the name of the accused. The minute books of jury (solemn) trials record the names and designations of jurors, though these remain un-indexed. However, when a juror failed to appear for an assize, then they themselves were subject to the force of law and the attention of the courts. In 1801, Robert Duff, esquire, of Muirtown, Inverness, was fined 100 merks Scots on 4 April 1801 for failure to appear for the assize at the High Court Inverness circuit (JC11/45, folio 1v). Such misdemeanours by jurors are recorded in the Justiciary trials catalogue.

Victims

14.22 Perhaps the most overlooked group among the records of criminal trials are those who were most directly affected by crime, namely the victims. Again, they are a hidden source for family history, owing to the previous practice of identifying criminal records by the name of the accused. The Justiciary trials catalogue records the names of many victims, though as yet it remains incomplete. From the Justiciary Court sitting papers (JC26), we discover that James Fraser of 32 Ann Street, Dundee, and Jane Lyall of 29 Rosebank Street, Dundee, were both victims of the crime of house-breaking as perpetrated by John Garrity. Garrity, who had a previous conviction for theft, was tried at the High Court Dundee circuit on 17 January 1890. He was found guilty and sentenced to 12 months' impris-onment with hard labour (JC26/1890/228).

Prisoners

14.23 Persons accused of crimes might, before the trial, be lodged in prison, as well as finding themselves there after sentence, either for a period of imprisonment or while waiting for transportation or hanging. Personal information about prisoners may be found in those prison registers which are preserved among the Home and Health Department records (HH).

14.24 Check the HH21 lists in the HH catalogue to see if there is a register of prisoners in a prison in which your ancestor might have been placed. Many of these registers only cover the 1840s to the 1870s. Some continue into the twentieth century and are closed for 75 years. Remember that, until 1880, civil debtors as well as those charged with or found guilty of crimes might be imprisoned. If the register is only of criminal prisoners, this is specified in the catalogue. Most of these registers supply the name, age, height, marital status, places of birth and residence, occupation and religion of each prisoner, as well as his crime, the court which tried him and the sentence.

14.25 Information about prisoners who were sentenced to transportation may be found in the register of a prison which served the court where they were tried, or in the registers of prisons in Aberdeen and Edinburgh where such prisoners waited to be moved to England. The records of the Edinburgh (Calton) Prison include a separate register of convicts under sentence of transportation from 1852 (HH21/5/16). This provides the name, age, crime, place of trial, marital status and trade of each prisoner, along with comments by the chaplain. As the ships which carried such prisoners to Australia sailed from England, further information about them is kept in the Home Office records in The National Archives in London. These Home Office records include convict transportation registers, 1787-1870, of which you may consult a microfilm copy in the NAS (RH4/160). These registers are arranged chronologically by date of departure of each ship. The last microfilm reel (RH4/160/7) includes a list of ships to each colony and an index of ships, showing the date and destination of each. The Scottish prisoners are placed near the end of the list of convicts on each ship. The information given is the name of the convict and where, when and for how many years he was sentenced. There could be a delay of several years between conviction and transportation. The last transportation ship to sail to Western Australia in 1867 carried Alex Casey, who had been sentenced to 15 years penal servitude in Edinburgh in 1858. A small series of transportation papers can also be found in the Justiciary Court records (JC41) for the period 1653 to 1853. The early period mainly consists of certificates of transportation of convicts to America in the 1770s. The receiving authorities returned a statement that the prisoners had landed. The later papers date from 1837 to 1853 and consist of lists of convicts to be transported and extract sentences of transportation.

14.26 Apart from the HH21 series, there are two further sets of prison registers of particular interest. HH11 is the reference number of the Edinburgh

Tolbooth Warding and Liberation Books, 1657–1816. These 39 volumes usually have a contents list under initial letters of surnames. They deal with both civil and criminal prisoners, stating their name and designation, at whose instance they are incarcerated and sometimes which court dealt with the case. Extracts from these records, 1657–1686, have been published in the *Book of the Old Edinburgh Club,* volumes 4–6, 8, 9, 11 and 12. The Liberation information may occasionally be of further use. For example, in October 1735, William Fowler, an Irishman, was incarcerated by a warrant of his employers, a firm of shipbuilders in Irvine, for theft. Three weeks later, he was liberated by warrant both of his employers and of the JPs 'who Indented with Mr Ferguson for the plantations' (HH11/18).

14.27 HH12 is a series of miscellaneous prison records, including records of prisoners in the condemned cell. The most valuable record in the series is a bound set of forms giving particulars of prisoners in Greenock Prison, 1872–1888 (HH12/56/7). Not only do these forms supply detailed personal information about each prisoner, but also added is a photograph of the prisoner in his or her best clothes.

Pardons and Remissions

14.28 A few criminals have the good fortune to have their crime pardoned or their sentence 'remitted'. Such remissions, often reducing a sentence of death to that of transportation, were granted by the Crown through the office of the Great Seal. If you are looking for a remission granted before 1668, use the published *Register of the Great Seal of Scotland* (see 10.23–25) and *Register of the Privy Seal of Scotland* (see 7.17). There is a modern typed index of remissions between 1668 and 1906 in the West Search Room. This supplies the name, sometimes designation, place of conviction and offence of each person, with the date of remission and volume and running number (not page number) of the Great Seal Paper Register. If you find your ancestor in this index, order out by C3 and the volume number, unless the volume number is preceded by a letter (eg S32), in which case refer to the introduction to the index for fresh advice. The index includes some remissions omitted from the Great Seal Register but surviving in other records. Remissions are granted for a wide variety of crimes, adultery and drunkenness as well as murder. In 1896, William Cochrane was remitted his five-shilling fine by the Glasgow Police Court for playing football on the street (C3/47, no 64). Until 1896, these remissions are in Latin. However, they do not contain much information not in the

Prisoners in Greenock Prison, 1873 (HH12/56/7)

index, never explaining why the remission was granted, but may be useful in leading you to the court records of the case.

14.29 Details of remitted sentences are also recorded in the High Court Books of Adjournal and Minute Books. In 1813, Robert McLaren, a labourer from Lochee, Forfar, was tried on 28 September 1813 at the High Court Perth circuit for the crime of theft by housebreaking. He was found guilty and sentenced to be hanged by the public executioner. On petition, the sentence of death was remitted under the Great Seal to transportation for 7 years and is recorded in the High Court minute book. (JC8/10, f. 45v). These details are recorded within the Justiciary trials catalogue. Copies of warrants of remissions, from 1682 to 1918, may be found in the Justiciary records under JC24. English versions of remissions between 1762 and 1849 may be found in RH2/4/255-273, which contains photostat copies of the Home Office Criminal Entry Books for Scotland (originals in The National Archives in London).

∞ 15 ∞

Taxpayers

15.1 Tax records have already been mentioned in respect of death duties (8.36–37) and land tax (10.36–38), which was also known as the cess.

15.2 Various other types of taxes were levied for varying periods of years. The lists of people liable for each tax or of payments made by them may be worth examining. At least, you may find that a person of a certain name was resident in a certain parish.

Hearth Tax

15.3 In 1690, Parliament granted a tax on every hearth in the kingdom. Both landowners and tenants were liable to pay and therefore may be named in the records of this tax, which date between 1691 and 1695, but have not all survived. Look at the catalogue referenced E69 and read the introduction. The records are arranged by counties. Within a county, look for a List of hearths or, not quite so useful, Accounts of hearth money collected (these may omit personal names). If you order out a list or account for your county, you will find it is arranged by parishes. Within parishes, there will be a list of those who had hearths in their houses, eg 'Georg Edgar tennent in Evelaw three [hearths], John Wilson coatter there one' (E69/5/1). Sometimes just the name of the hearth-owner is given, without designation. There is a supplementary series of hearth tax records for the same period in the Leven and Melville Muniments. Look up the GD26 inventory at references GD26/7/300-391. Lists of hearths in some Ross-shire parishes are in the Cromartie Muniments (GD305/1/64, nos 240-1, 243, 271-2, 277, 280-1).

Poll Tax

15.4 Poll taxes were imposed on Scotland between 1693 and 1699 on all adults except those dependent on charity. Unfortunately, the records are not complete. Look in the catalogue referenced E70. This lists two series of records, each arranged by counties; the E70 series itself and a supplementary list of poll-tax records surviving in other record groups. This latter list also notes some printed versions. Having read the introduction, look at both lists under the relevant county. These describe assorted lists and accounts of pollable persons, the information, which is variable, again collected within parishes. At their most informative, these records can be genealogically useful, naming children and servants, eg 'James Rutherfurde Tennent in Sawchtan for himself, his wife, Wm, Janet and Elizat his children' (E70/8/1 – Account for parish of Crichton in Midlothian).

Post-Union Taxes

15.5 From 1748, certain assessed taxes were levied in Scotland and copies of the lists (schedules) of people assessed to pay have been preserved among the Exchequer records. Look at the E326 catalogue and read first the general introduction and the introductions to the individual tax records. The records of each tax are arranged by counties, as described in the catalogue, and within counties by parishes (not in alphabetical order), but royal burghs are listed separately – check the catalogue carefully.

15.6 Window Tax, 1748-1798 (E326/1), Commutation Tax, 1784-1798 (E326/2), Inhabited House Tax, 1778-1798 (E326/3) and Consolidated Assessed Taxes, 1798-1799 (E326/15) were all taxes on householders (owners or tenants, one per dwelling house). However, this record is not as useful as it sounds, as only the better-off were taxed. A house had to have at least seven windows or a rent of at least £5 yearly before it was liable for tax. In some rural parishes, the only persons liable for tax were the minister and a couple of lairds. The schedules for burghs and some more populous parishes are useful in listing more names, but omission of designations and of locations of the dwelling houses limits their usefulness. The schedule for the burgh of Aberdeen in 1773 lists 546 window-tax-paying inhabitants, but they include five ladies described simply as 'Mrs Forbes' (E326/1/128).

15.7 A shop tax was levied between 1785 and 1789. If you want to find if your ancestor had a shop worth a rental of more than £5 per year at that time, look at E326/4. Unfortunately, the business is not always specified.

15.8 Taxes were levied on certain classes of servants, mainly domestic (male servants, 1777-1798, E326/5, and female, 1785-1792, E326/6). While you may want to find out how many servants your well-off ancestor employed, the schedules of these taxes are more significant in that they usually name the servants, sometimes also stating what kind of servant, and in that the record notes which masters were bachelors as they had to pay double tax. In Earlston parish in 1778, Captain Colin Falconer's footman was 'Osemin a Negro' (E326/5/1).

15.9 The other assessed taxes, on carts, carriages, horses, dogs and clocks and watches, all for brief periods of years up to 1798, are, with one exception, of little added use. The exception is Farm Horse Tax (1797-1798, E326/10), which is continued in the Consolidated Assessed Taxes (1798-1799, E326/15). Its value is that it helps to identify tenant farmers. In the parish of Strathdon in 1799, three persons paid window tax, five more paid house tax, but another 47 paid farm horse tax (E326/15/1). It is unfortunate that this record covers such a short period of time, being continued only for Midlothian up to 1812 (E327/36-54).

Excerpt from Edinburgh inhabited House Tax, 1778, giving names and occupations of householders (E326/3/40).

15.10 Income tax was first imposed in 1799 on annual incomes of £60 and over. Lists of those who made returns survive for Midlothian, 1799-1801 (E327/18-31), and for certain other counties and burghs (see the catalogue) for 1801-1802 (E326/14). One point of interest here is that abatements were made on account of children. If the number of children is not stated, it should be possible to calculate this from the sum deducted. The rules for such abatements are contained in the Duties on Income Act, 1778.

15.11 Income tax was replaced in 1803 by a property tax assessed on income from ownership and occupation of land, investments, trades and offices. The Exchequer records contain records for Midlothian only, 1803-1812 (E327/78-121). The trades and offices of taxpayers are specified, particularly in Edinburgh, where the arrangement is by street within parish. Natale Corri at the Concert Hall was assessed as making a profit in 1803 of £200 from his trade as a musician (E327/81).

∽ *16* ∽

Officials

16.1 The highest-ranking government officials are listed in the *Handbook of British Chronology* (Royal Historical Society, London). The appointments of other officials may be found in the records of the Great and Privy Seal: officials such as sheriffs and other judges, lieutenants of counties, keepers of registers of sasines, sheriff and commissary clerks. Indexes of such commissions, both of persons and of offices, are available from 1668 to 1955 (Great Seal) and from 1660 to 1898 (Privy Seal, English record). Most of these Great Seal commissions are ordered out by the reference C3 and the volume number, but not all – first check the introductory pages to the index. Privy Seal commissions are ordered out by PS3 and the volume number. For earlier commissions, you should use the printed Great and Privy Seal volumes, except for the Privy Seal record between 1585 and 1660 when you should use a list referenced PS7/1 which leads you to the entries in volumes referenced PS1. If your ancestor is unexpectedly absent from these records or you want more information about his appointment, try the records mentioned in 16.2-3.

16.2 Lists of the holders of some of these minor offices (including HM Limner, the Historiographer-Royal and Governors of Edinburgh Castle) are available in the Historical Search Room (library reference 334). Adjacent on the shelf is a typed volume (library reference 332) 'Civil and Judicial Establishment 1707-1830'. This is a copy of an Exchequer record (E229/10/1) that lists the holders of various offices, including the staffs of the Courts of Exchequer, Justiciary and Session. Unfortunately, this record is incomplete. Gaps may be filled by checking the appropriate Court records themselves. For example, the Lord Advocate, as crown representative and chief prosecutor in Scotland, would appoint advocates on a temporary basis to act as his representative or depute. Such appointees would present their commission of appointment at the first appropriate court sitting date. Therefore we see that on 2 April 1799, John Burnett, Esquire, advocate, was appointed as Advocate Depute to prosecute cases in the High Court for the duration of the Spring (South) circuit (JC12/23, f. 1r). Such appointments, both permanent and temporary, are recorded in the Justiciary trials catalogue against the relevant minute book entry.

16.3 Government officials had to be paid and, as a result, post-Union bureaucracy produced several series of Exchequer records, which give information of the appointments and salaries of officials after 1707. These records overlap considerably and are not consistent throughout each series. It is not immediately apparent why information may be in one record and not another. The following are the most useful and are all in volume form. Look at the relevant catalogue for dates and call numbers of each volume. In these volumes there are indexes or contents lists of commissions and warrants, but no indexes of the persons named in the salary lists. Some also contain records of other payments, including Civil List pensions (i.e. annuities to worthy persons in need), so that you may find there an ancestor who received an income from the government, even if not employed by them: but look first at the index to the Privy Seal English Record (PS3) for such pensioners.

E313   Copies of commissions and warrants for paying salaries etc, 1709-1965.

E224   Establishment entry books containing lists of salaries and pensions, 1709-1866, and warrants thereof, 1709-1834. Judges and court officials will be found throughout; later volumes include staffs of government boards and of Register House. The last list in which a person appears will often provide the date on which he died or left office.

E810   Lists of salaries, superannuations, and pensions, 1854-1930. Useful range of recipients.

E811   Lists of salaries, 1869-1930. Include staffs of the Exchequer, court offices, Register House, boards and commissions.

16.4 A government employee may of course be mentioned in the records of the department in which he was employed and therefore it may be worth checking establishment or staff records in the catalogue of that department's records. For example, if your ancestor was employed in the General Register Office for Scotland between 1909 and 1920, he should appear in the files referenced GRO5/774–776. However, in most of these departmental records, records of staff do not start until well into the twentieth century and do not include personal files. The staff of three government organisations before 1900 are, however, well recorded – the

Board of Customs, the Board of Excise, and the Post Office. Bear in mind that data protection issues may apply if you are looking for more recent staff records.

16.5 A separate Scottish Board of Customs functioned from 1707 until 1829. Look in the CE catalogue at CE3 and CE12 for establishment books. These contain quarterly lists, arranged by port, of all Customs officers, except junior clerks and the crews of the Excise vessels known as 'cutters' (commanders and mates are named). Payments of salaries to Customs officers are recorded in the Customs cash accounts (E502). The date payment stopped would be the date of death, dismissal or resignation. If your ancestor was a Customs officer in the mid-eighteenth century, look at two further records, GD1/372/1 and RH2/8/102, which list the officers in 1752 and 1755, arranged by port and supplying for each his age and character (eg, 'A tipler, Indolent, & not capable' or 'Capable & Sober. Worn out in the Service'). GD1/372/1 valuably also records his birthplace, whether he has a wife and how many children.

16.6 The separate Scottish Board of Excise survived until 1830. Its records are also listed in the CE catalogue. Mr J F Mitchell gathered information about the Excise officers between 1707 and 1830 from this and other sources and noted it on cards arranged alphabetically. These cards may be consulted in the NAS on microfilm (RH4/6/1-2). The information is supplied in rather succinct form, and therefore you should first read the explanation of the arrangement of the symbols on the cards which appears at the beginning of the microfilm. Although Mitchell searched widely, the information on his cards is not exclusive. You may find further details, or simply prefer to search first, in:

GD1/54/10, which includes a list of Excise officers in 1743

CE6/19, which lists all officers in 1794 under the initial letter of each's surname, stating his age and the number of his family, or

CE13/1-9, which is a series of volumes minuting the appointments and removals of Excise staff between 1813 and 1829. The CE13 volumes are indexed by initial letter of surnames, then by order of appearance in the book.

16.7 The Post Office records contain a series of establishment books, listing the salaried staff, from 1803 to 1911 (PO1/15-65). These books are arranged by post-towns, naming all the staff in the main post offices, including letter carriers, but do not name sub-postmasters. PO1/16, which records postal staff in 1803, notes their dates of appointment (eg Margaret MacKerchar was appointed to Aberfeldy in 1799) and also has later annotations.

∽ 17 ∾

Soldiers, Sailors and Airmen

17.1 After 1707, the Army and Navy were administered from London. Therefore, if you are seeking information about an ancestor's military or naval service after 1707, or air service in the twentieth century, you should apply to The National Archives (formerly the Public Record Office) which holds War Office, Admiralty and Air Force records. Even before the Union, references in the records to named individuals in the Scottish army and navy are sparse (particularly the navy). Nevertheless, there are records in the NAS that may be of use to you. Further to those described below, you should look at the source lists of military records and naval and mercantile records.

Soldiers before 1707

17.2 The main record of individuals in the Scottish army is the Muster Rolls which are in the Exchequer records. Look at the catalogue referenced E100. These muster rolls are arranged by regiment and, within regiment, by companies or troops. Though the earliest is dated 1641, most are dated after 1680. They name all the officers and men in a troop or company at a certain place and date. Ranks are stated, except for troopers. Few rolls supply any other information. Your problem is that unless you already know that your ancestor was in a particular regiment, you may have to look through some 4,800 rolls in the hope of finding him. It may help you that many recruits came from the estates owned by their Colonel or his family and most regiments were known by the name of their commanding officer (eg Lord Jedburgh's dragoons). Some of these rolls are printed in *The Scots Army, 1661-1688* by C Dalton (republished in 1989 by Greenhill Books), but only officers appear in the book's index. Similar lists of those serving in particular regiments may be found in GD collections (see 6.19-20), where a member of that family had been granted a commission to be Colonel of a regiment.

17.3 If your ancestor was an officer, there is more likely to be a record of him, than if he were a common soldier. Commissions in the army were granted by the Crown and, from 1670, some were recorded in the Warrant Books of the Secretary of Scotland, along with other government business. Look up the State Papers catalogue at SP4 to find the volume covering the relevant dates. These volumes each contain a contents list or index. The commissions supply only the name, rank, company and regiment of the officer, no other personal details. These SP4 commissions are noted and indexed in Dalton's *The Scots Army, 1661-1688* and thereafter in his *English Army Lists and Commission Registers, 1661-1714*. There is also a small series of commissions, 1643, 1689-1827, in RH9/9 – look up that catalogue; and commissions may occasionally be found in GD collections.

Soldiers after 1707

17.4 The only military records after the Union among public records in the NAS are those of the Militia and more recently the Territorials.

17.5 Though Militia records run from the 1790s to the mid-nineteenth century, the heyday of the Militia force was the Napoleonic Wars. These records have two main points of genealogical interest: they name the young men who were balloted to serve in the Militia and they name some of their wives. Look in the catalogue of Sheriff Court (SC) or County Council (CO) records of the sheriffdom or county in which your ancestor lived. The relevant records, if they survive, will be catalogued under the heading of Lieutenancy and/or Militia or Miscellaneous. They usually appear near the end of an SC catalogue. A list of references to militia records is printed in J Gibson and M Medlycott's *Militia Lists and Musters 1757-1876* (Federation of Family History Societies, 1994).

17.6 As conscription was by ballot, only some men were made to serve. The militiamen had to be healthy and between 18 and 30, until 1802, thereafter between 18 and 45. Certain categories were exempted, including apprentices and poor men with more than two children (see the Militia (Scotland) Act 1802 (s.38)). Despite these limitations, the Militia records by name many people whose existence might not otherwise be recorded. In the Highland parish of Braemar and Crathie in 1800, 60 young men were listed (CO6/5/6). Information about individual militiamen appears in the schedules of those eligible to be balloted (some claiming exemption), in lists of men conscripted, and in minute books. The basic infor-

Application by wife of militiaman for financial support, 1805 (SC29/72/2).

mation supplied about a militiaman is his name, profession and place of abode, but sometimes his age is stated and, more rarely, place of birth. Thus we know that Charles Herkes aged 22, a weaver in Dunbar in 1825, was born in County Down (CO7/13/2).

17.7 When a man was serving in the Militia and his family were unable to support themselves, his wife and children under 10 years of age were eligible for an allowance. Records of claims for such allowances appear amongst Lieutenancy and Militia records. These name each wife and, usually but not invariably, her husband; say how many children, sometimes naming them; and state the parish where she lived. An additional record of such payments to wives and children in Midlothian, 1803-1815, is contained in the Exchequer records (E327/147-158).

17.8 Some militia records may be found in the GD series (see 6.19-20). For example, the Seaforth Muniments include lists of men between 15 and 60 able to bear arms in parishes in Ross-shire in 1798 (GD46/6/45).

17.9 The Ministry of Defence records in the NAS consist of Territorial and Auxiliary Forces Associations' records. These include a list of members of Dundee Volunteer Rifle Corps in 1859 (MD7/1), a muster roll of the 5th Forfarshire Volunteer Corps 1859-1886 (MD7/2), which gives the ages, occupations, and residences of the volunteers, and a list of members of the Dundee National Reserve in 1914 (MD7/3). The rest of the MD records are all post-1900 and mostly minute books. While officers are regularly named in them, other ranks are rarely named.

17.10 The wills and inventories of servicemen of all services and ranks could be recorded in the normal way, and for the period from 1876 onwards can be found in the Calendar of Confirmations (see Chapter 8.) There is also a separate series of soldiers' wills, mainly covering the First and Second World Wars, with a few pre-1914, for the inter-war years and the post-war period to 1966 (SC70/8). These records are only for soldiers up to the rank of sergeant who were domiciled in Scotland. Their wills were sent to the Commissary Office in Edinburgh by the War Office in terms of section 21 of the Regimental Debts Act 1893.

17.11 The wills for the First World War are arranged in the batches in which they were sent, usually many months after the soldier's death. By the end of December 1919 the Commissary Office had received almost 25,000 wills. There is no index to the whole series, but there are lists of each batch, starting with the first one dated 3 June 1915 (SC70/9). Within each batch the wills are arranged by the letter of the alphabet and a running number under each letter. The lists of wills include the helpful details of name, regimental number, rank unit and date of death. They also give the date on which the wills were sent by the War Office, and the running number under each letter, which enable you to look up the relevant reference number in the catalogue of SC70/8.

17.12 The wills for the Second World War are arranged in numbered batches, known as 'lists'. To find a will you can check the alphabetical card index (SC70/9). This gives the soldier's name and other service details, the number and date of the list in which the will occurs, and the War Department's will reference. You can then look up the catalogue of SC70/8 and find the reference matching the will reference number.

17.13 Soldiers in both world wars mostly made use of the Army's official printed forms, but occasionally they wrote their own will, sometimes in the form of a personal letter. Some wills are signed and witnessed, but the 'informal will' form in the pay book and forms used for soldiers on active service during the Second World War did not require a witness. Normally they were authenticated posthumously by an officer. The personal details which you can find in the wills include the soldier's name, War Office numbers, regimental number, rank, unit, the date and details of his bequest (usually very simple), the named beneficiary or beneficiaries and their home address, and the date and place of death.

17.14 For further details of a soldier's service records you should consult The National Archives in London.

Sailors

17.15 There are no official records of the Scottish navy, as such. There are a few miscellaneous naval documents in the Exchequer records: see list E90. The most useful of these are printed in *The Old Scots Navy, 1689-1710* by James Grant. Those apart, information about Scottish ships and the men who sailed in them has to be gleaned from the various records of Scottish government, such as the Privy Council.

Merchant Seamen

17.16 Though both before and after 1707 the Customs Accounts record the movement of ships in and out of ports, they do not record the names of crew or passengers. Only the master or captain of the ship is named. These Customs Accounts are referenced E71 (for the period up to 1640), E72 (1662-1696) and E504 (1742-1830). They are arranged by ports.

17.17 The crews of ships engaged in whale fishing between 1750 and 1825 are named in the vouchers of payments of bounties (E508/47/8-130/8). The ships, ports and owners are named in the Customs cash accounts (E5021 48-130), which provide a key to the individual vouchers. Similarly, the crews of ships engaged in herring fishing between 1752 and 1796 are named in the more numerous vouchers for herring bounties (E508/49/9-96/9). Here again the cash accounts (E502) record ships, owners and ports, which should lead you to the voucher you want.

17.18 Seamen who used the port of Leith may be found in the records of Trinity House of Leith (GD226), a mutual benefit society for the support of the poor, aged and infirm mariners and their dependents. Minute and cash books date from the mid-seventeenth century and record payments by seamen as well as pensions to them and their dependents, mainly widows. Included are records of the pilots who guided ships into the harbour.

17.19 Since 1835, it has been compulsory for masters of ships to enter into agreements with any crew member before sailing. Not all records of such agreements have been kept. A small number, dating between 1867 and 1913 and relating to Scottish ships, are preserved in the NAS. Look up the catalogue referenced BT3. If this record fails you, you should try the crew lists in the Glasgow City Archives, The National Archives in London, the National Maritime Museum in London and the Memorial University, Newfoundland. These crew agreements supply the name, age and birthplace of each seaman. To search this record, you need to know the name of the ship in which your ancestor might have sailed.

17.20 Soldiers and sailors occasionally fell foul of the law and appeared in the criminal courts. Entries for High Court criminal trials may include regiment and rank of the person, or the vessel on which they served. For example, we find that Edward Bagnet Harvey O'Keeffe, Lieutenant, 21st Regiment of Foot and Godfrey Margery, Ensign, 3rd North British or Lanarkshire Militia were both indicted at Perth in April 1801 for murder by duelling. Having failed to appear for trial they were declared outlaws (JC11/45, f. 24v). The Justiciary trials catalogue records these men and the outcome of such trials.

Airmen

17.21 A small, separate series of airmen's wills exists for the period 1941-1950 (SC70/10). These are arranged by date of receipt of the wills in the Commissary Office. Some of the wills include a Service and Pay Book, which can provide details of date of birth, civilian occupation, religion, marital status, terms of service, and service history.

17.22 For further details of RAF service records you should consult The National Archives in London.

∽ 18 ∽

Clergymen and Church Members

Presbyterian Ministers

18.1 If your ancestor was a Presbyterian clergyman who had a parish or congregation, then look for him in one of the following printed sources.

Fasti Ecclesiae Scoticanae. This series of volumes provides biographical, including family, details of all known ministers of the established Church of Scotland since the Reformation. Some omissions from early volumes are corrected in volume 8. As much of the information in the *Fasti* was based on record research, it may be worth following up references given in particular biographies.

History of the Congregations of the United Presbyterian Church, 1733-1900.

Annals and Statistics of the Original Secession Church. This book is not indexed.

Annals of the Free Church of Scotland, 1843-1900.

The Fasti of the United Free Church of Scotland, 1900-1929.

These last four publications contain information about the main denominations which dissented from the Church of Scotland in the eighteenth and nineteenth centuries. Additional details will be found in the records of the churches and presbyteries in which these men served (see CH catalogues). Information about some dissenting ministers may be found in their Friendly Society records (CH3/515-517). CH3/515/8, a list of Relief Synod ministers, gives the dates of birth, marriage and death of them and their wives.

18.2 You may find references to students of divinity in the minutes of the presbyteries and synods (CH2 and 3) in which they were probationers.

Some are mentioned briefly in the mainly nineteenth century records of theological colleges and student societies (CH3/119, CH3/273, CH3/281, CH3/305, CH3/885).

18.3 It may be difficult to find a record of a Presbyterian clergyman who did not succeed in obtaining a church in Scotland. Some, between 1725 and 1876, may have been appointed itinerant preachers and catechists within the Highlands and Islands and, as such, appear in the records of the Royal Bounty Committee of the General Assembly of the Church of Scotland (CH1/5/51-79). These records are unindexed but include marginal tags and occasional lists of the catechists. Some missionaries and catechists had their salaries paid by the Society in Scotland for Propagating Christian Knowledge (see 19.6) and are named in the SSPCK's scheme ledgers (GD95/7). Records of Presbyterian missionaries abroad are preserved in the National Library of Scotland.

Other Clergymen

18.4 Two useful reference works are *Scottish Episcopal Clergy, 1689–2000* by David M Bertie (T & T Clark, 2000) and *The Scottish Congregational Ministry, 1794–1993* by William D McNaughton (Congregational Union of Scotland, 1993). In the absence of published biographical details, information about non-Presbyterian clergymen must be sought in the records of their churches (try the CH catalogues) or by enquiring of their present-day church headquarters.

18.5 Roman Catholic priests, 1732-1878, are listed in *The Innes Review* (Scottish Catholic Historical Association), volumes 17, 34 and 40. Registers of student priests at the Scots Colleges at Douai, Rome, Madrid, Valladolid and Ratisbon are printed and indexed in *Records of Scots Colleges* (New Spalding Club, 1906). The information is in Latin, but often includes the age and parentage of the student. The NAS has a photocopy of the register of the College in Rome 1602-1939 (RH2/7/14) and a microfilm copy of the registers of the College at Douai 1581-1772 (RH4/18). Further enquiries about Roman Catholic priests might be made to the Scottish Catholic Archives (address in Appendix A).

Presbyterian Church Members

18.6 Not until the mid-nineteenth-century did it become common for church records to include lists of church members ('communicants') or to record the names of those who joined that church. Such information is sometimes contained in separate volumes – look in the list of records of the church in question in the CH catalogue for a communion roll, list of communicants, list of parishioners, roll of male heads of families, etc. Such lists sometimes tell if a communicant came from another parish. Lists of communicants are sometimes inscribed in the kirk session minute books, particularly lists of young communicants on their joining the Kirk. The names of those who rented seats in a church may appear in account books.

18.7 In seventeenth and eighteenth century kirk session records, you will find the names of elders, those in receipt of poor relief, and those accused of or witness to scandalous behaviour (most commonly fornication, but it could be shoeing a horse on the Sabbath). Otherwise parishioners are not usually named, even when they move into the parish. But one cannot be

List of Roman Catholics in the parish of Buittle, 1704 (CH1/2/5/3, no. 197/1).

categorical about this: for example, the earliest minute book of Linlithgow kirk session (CH2/740/1) records testimonials brought by incomers to the parish, 1645-1647.

Roman Catholics

18.8 Between 1700 and 1714, the names of Roman Catholics in their parishes were listed by Church of Scotland ministers and these lists of 'papists' are preserved among the records of the General Assembly of the Church of Scotland. Look in the CH catalogue at CH1/2/5 and CH1/2/29-34 for the reference numbers of lists of Catholics in the parishes in which your ancestors dwelt.

18.9 For more recent members of the Roman Catholic faith, look at the index of churches at the start of the RH21 catalogue and then at the records of a relevant church to see if they include a register of communicants or confirmations. The earliest of these date from 1749, but the majority are nineteenth century.

Members of Other Churches

18.10 Look at the CH catalogue to see if the records of a particular church are in the NAS. Check the list of these records to see if they include a roll of members or communion roll: failing which look at minutes or other records. Among the Episcopalian records there are lists of communicants in the dioceses of Ross, Caithness and Argyll in 1762 and 1770 (CH12/1/12).

⤳ 19 ⤳

Schoolmasters and Scholars

19.1 The Education (Scotland) Act, 1872, was a watershed in the history of schooling in Scotland. The records which you should investigate for teachers are in the main different before and after that Act, though the ones mentioned in 19.6,19.8 and 19.10 overlap 1872 to some extent. As there are many books about individual schools or education in particular areas and many of the relevant records are preserved in the region or district where the school was, you should first investigate the sources in the local library or record office. Within the NAS, look also at the three source lists on education. Source list no.17 is incomplete but will refer you to relevant records in some GD collections. To trace your schoolmaster's name in the records suggested below will often involve searching unindexed minute books, some of which will have helpful marginal annotations (eg 'Ja: Turnbull schoolmaster'), some not.

Schoolmasters and Scholars

19.2 The majority of schoolmasters taught in the parish or burgh school. You will find appointments of burgh schoolmasters recorded in the burgh or town council minutes. Look up the name of the burgh in the index to the B repertory, and in the list of records of that burgh look for the council minutes. For example, in 1690 the council of the burgh of Dunbar nominated James Turnbull, youngest lawful son to the deceased George Turnbull, merchant burgess of that burgh, to be schoolmaster 'for learning the Childrein to read, wryt, lay compts and work arthmetick' (B18/13/2, f.34v).

19.3 Parish schoolmasters were nominated by the heritors (i.e. landowners) and minister of the parish and usually were then examined by the presbytery to ensure that they were qualified for the post. The record of the appointment of a parish schoolmaster should be in the Heritors Records. Look up the name of the parish in the index to the HR catalogue, and in the list of records for that parish look for the heritors' minutes. If no heritors' records survive for the required parish and date, then you should search the CH2 records of that parish and the relevant presbytery. The kirk session records for the parish may contain the name of a schoolmaster, particularly as the schoolmaster often acted as session clerk. The presbytery minute books should record the presbytery's confirmation of the appointment of a schoolmaster. In the Church of Scotland, a presbytery is the court superior to the kirk session. The *Fasti Ecclesiae Scoticanae* (see 18.1) will tell you which presbytery includes the parish in which you are interested.

19.4 The kirks of the Free Church of Scotland, which was founded in 1843, often set up their own schools. To find the record of the appointment of a teacher of a Free Church school, look up the name of the kirk in the CH3 catalogue and then the list of that kirk's records. Order out the Deacons' Court minutes (rather than the Session minutes), as the deacons appointed and paid the teacher.

19.5 Schoolmasters may appear in other records. The records of a parliamentary commission in 1690 include some lists of schoolmasters. Those in the counties of Angus, Berwickshire, East Lothian, Fife, Midlothian, Peebleshire, Perthshire, Roxburghshire and Stirlingshire (PA10/2) are printed in the Scottish History Society 4th series volume 2 *Miscellany* X. There is a list for Ayrshire among papers referenced PA10/5.

19.6 Paradoxically, concern at the scarcity of schools in the Highlands and Islands led to a better recording of the schoolmasters who taught there. In the eighteenth and nineteenth centuries, the Society in Scotland for Propagating Christian Knowledge (SSPCK) erected and maintained schools in the Highlands, Islands and Remote Corners of Scotland where 'popery and ignorance' did 'much abound'. More information can be found in *SSPCK Schoolmasters, 1709–1872* edited by A S Cowper (Scottish Record Society, 1997). To view the records of the Society, look at the GD95 catalogue. While the Society's minute books, letter books and inspectors' reports mention teachers, you will find the names of the SSPCK teachers more quickly in the register of schools, 1710-1761 (GD95/9/1); salary books, 1766-1779 (GD95/8/5); scheme ledgers, 1771-1890 (GD95/7); and abstract of school returns, 1827-1878 (GD95/9/6-7). Some of these records are arranged by presbyteries.

19.7 The SSPCK appointed its own teachers, to supplement the parish schoolmasters appointed by the heritors. There are three other records which provide further information about the parish schoolmasters in the Highlands and Islands. The Commissioners who until 1784 administered the estates forfeited after the 1745 Jacobite rising were heritors of the parishes in which these estates lay and therefore the records of their administration include the names of schoolmasters. There is a location list of the estates by county and parish at the beginning of the catalogue of their records (E700-788). Look up 'schools' in the index to the catalogue and also look at the various reports on particular estates (E729 etc), some of which are printed (and indexed) in *Reports on the Annexed Estates, 1755-1769* edited by Virginia Wills (HMSO, 1973).

19.8 By his will, a Mr James Dick set up a trust for the maintenance and assistance of the parochial (not burgh) schoolmasters in the counties of Aberdeen, Banff and Moray. If your ancestor was a teacher in these counties after 1832, look in the inventory of the Dick Bequest Trust records (GD1/4).

19.9 In terms of the Highlands Schools Act, 1838, the Treasury had to provide funds for additional schools in the Highlands. If your ancestor was a Highland schoolmaster between 1840 and 1863, look at the volumes referenced E224/32-40. The entry 'Schools, Schedule of Grants to' in the index to each volume will lead you to the list of schoolmasters who benefited from this fund.

19.10 In 1847, the Educational Institute of Scotland, a professional association for teachers, was formed. Its records, which contain the names of many teachers who joined its ranks, also include the records of earlier mutual benefit societies formed by teachers in Glasgow (1794-1836), Roxburgh (1811-1840) and Jedburgh (1824-1872). Look at the inventory of the Institute's records (GD342).

19.11 The Department of Education records include two volumes of reports by school inspectors before 1872. These are for the years 1859 (ED16/13) and 1866-1867 (ED16/14). Each volume reports on only a selection of schools, but they are indexed. Each report names the teacher and pupil-teachers of that school. Occasionally, an assistant teacher is named.

Schoolmasters since 1872

19.12 From 1872, school boards administered education at a parish level and records of the appointment of teachers and pupil-teachers are in the minute books of these school boards. School board records are mostly preserved among the records of their county council. The county council records presently held by the NAS, which include school board records, are those of Midlothian (CO2/105-129), East Lothian (CO7/5/2) and Dumfries-shire (Mouswald only, CO9/2/1). The East Lothian records also include school logbooks that mention teachers (CO7/5/4). There are a few school board minutes elsewhere in the NAS – Barra (SC29/75/3), Dervaig (SC59/15/4), Kilninian and Kilmore (SC59/15/1-3), North Berwick (B56/14), Prestonkirk (B18/18/12) and Stornoway (SC33/60). For other school board records, you should enquire at the relevant local record office, archive centre or library.

19.13 The records of the Scottish Education Department include school in-spection reports (ED16-18). These rarely name individuals, but can be of value in giving a general picture of the school your ancestor taught at or attended. Of the reports, the most useful are referenced ED16/1-12, as, although they report on only a limited number of schools between 1896

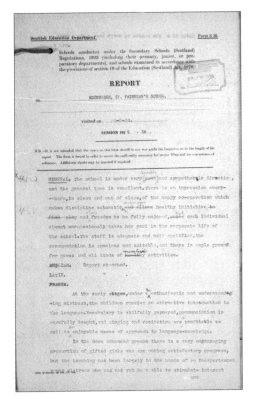

Report on St Trinnean's school, 1936 (ED32/105).

and 1909, the reports supply the names of the teachers and pupil-teachers at these schools. Some volumes include an index of schools. ED17 and ED18 have the advantage that there is a separate file for each school, clearly stated in the ED catalogue with separate reference number, but the disadvantage that teachers are often not named or named just by their surname (eg 'Mr Cormack'). Some closure periods apply on these records.

School Pupils and Students

19.14 Records of school pupils are rare. Some happen to be noted in school log books. As mentioned above, pupil-teachers (who existed between 1846 and 1906 and had to be at least 13 years old) are named in school board records and inspection reports. Leaving certificate registers, which give particulars of every school candidate, exist from 1908 (ED36), but are closed for 75 years.

19.15 The records of George Heriot's School, Edinburgh, are held by the NAS and include admission registers of its boy pupils, 1659-1939 (GD421, section 10). The NAS also has the records of Dr Guthrie's Schools (see 28.25).

19.16 Information about students of further education is best sought from the university or college they attended. Check printed sources first, as some lists of students are published. The NAS holds records of one such institution, the Edinburgh School (later College) of Art. These records include lists of applicants and students in the years 1828-1830 and 1848-1863. Look up the catalogue reference NG2/1. The lists of applicants for admission give the name, age (which could be as young as 12), profession and address of the applicant; and the lists of students, in addition to that information, give the name of the student's father.

Professors

19.17 Information about university staff is again best sought from that university. However, the appointments of some professors will be found in the Privy Seal records – look at the index to the Privy Seal English Record, 1660-1898 (PS3) – and also in the Exchequer records described in 16.3.

20

Medical Professions

Doctors

20.1 Since 1858, all medical practitioners in the United Kingdom have had to be registered. The NAS holds the original register of doctors in Scotland (CMC1/2), which you are welcome to consult, but the information therein is more easily obtained from *The Medical Register* that is published annually and may be consulted in large public libraries. This publication names all registered doctors alphabetically, along with their addresses and qualifications. Remember that some doctors who registered in 1858 had been practising for many years, including William Arrott, doctor in Arbroath, whose qualifications were 'Doctor of Medicine of the University of St Andrews 1798 and Licentiate of the Royal College of Surgeons of Edinburgh 1795'. In the early entries in CMC1/2, some dates of death are later annotated. Another annual publication which contains fuller biographical information about medical practitioners is *The Medical Directory*. There is a separate *Medical Directory for Scotland, 1852-1860*. Scottish doctors appear in the *London and Provincial Medical Directory, 1861-1869*, and thereafter in *The Medical Directory*.

20.2 For information about physicians and surgeons who had ceased to practise by 1858, you should apply to the Royal College of Physicians of Edinburgh, the Royal College of Surgeons of Edinburgh or the Royal College of Physicians and Surgeons of Glasgow (addresses in Appendix A).

Other Medical Personnel

20.3 In the Home and Health Department records, there are registers of nurses, including those working in poorhouses, between 1885 and 1930. The reference numbers are HH2/33-37.

20.4 There are published annual registers of chemists (from 1869), dentists (from 1879), midwives (from 1917) and nurses (from 1921). Though the NAS has a copy of the Midwives Roll for Scotland (CMB3) and the manuscript original of the Nurses' Register (GNC12), you may find it easier to consult the published volumes in a library.

21

Lawyers

21.1 There were two principal categories of lawyers in Scotland: advocates, who alone could plead in the supreme court, the Court of Session; and solicitors, who used to be known as writers and may also be known as law agents. Law agents who plead cases in sheriff and other inferior courts may be called procurators. Judges are usually appointed from the ranks of advocates. If your ancestor was a lawyer, first examine published sources. Judges of the Court of Session up to 1832 are described in Brunton and Haig's *Senators of the College of Justice*. Advocates are listed in *The Faculty of Advocates, 1532-1943* (Scottish Record Society). Many solicitors or writers are listed in *The Register of the Society of Writers to Her Majesty's Signet* (The Society of Writers to the Signet). The procurators in Aberdeen, who confusingly called themselves advocates, are listed in the *History of the Society of Advocates in Aberdeen* (New Spalding Club, 1912). All of these books contain genealogical information. The names of lawyers also appear in various published law lists or directories, notably the *Scottish Law List* which was previously called *Index Juridicus* and which dates from 1848. Many of the lawyers who practised in Edinburgh in the eighteenth century are mentioned in the notes to *Boswell's Edinburgh Journals, 1767-1786* edited by Hugh Milne (Mercat Press, 2001).

21.2 If you have exhausted the printed sources and want to examine the records in the NAS, remember that sheriffs and other judges are appointed and paid by government and therefore you might try the records mentioned in 16.1-3. Evidence of the professional career of judges, advocates and procurators will be found in the records of the court in which they operated. The Books of Sederunt of the Court of Session (CS1) contain copies of the appointments of the Lords of Session (i.e. the judges) and court officers and of the admission of advocates. The records of many sheriff courts include lists of procurators authorised to plead in that court, particularly since 1874 but in some courts since the end of the eighteenth century. Look in the contents list of the catalogue of the sheriff court for

159

'Register of Procurators' or 'Roll of Law Agents' or similar title: which failing, check under the miscellaneous section. These rolls are sometimes indexed and will usually give you the business address of the lawyer. (Some sheriff courts also keep registers of sheriff officers, who are appointed by the sheriff to enforce court decrees, but who are not lawyers.)

21.3 Many writers/solicitors are also notaries and thereby authorised to certify certain legal documents. The NAS holds the Register of Admission of Notaries (NP2), which starts in 1563 but is not a consistent record until 1661 and, as a register, stops in 1873. The warrants of admission of notaries fill some of the early gaps (NP3) and replace the Register from 1873 (NP5). If you are looking for a notary before 1680 look first at the chronological list in NP3/1. This list covers the years 1577-1591, 1619-1623 and 1672. For other years before 1680 you will have to go straight to the Register (NP2). Between 1680 and 1792, look at the partly alphabetical chronological list NP6/1, which gives the name, designation and date of admission of each notary. Order out the NP2 volume that includes that date. Between 1792 and 1873, you have to order out the appropriate NP2 volume and look at the index in it. Notaries admitted between 1873 and 1903 are listed briefly in NP6/2.

21.4 All the entries in the Register of Notaries give the name and designation of the notary. Some of the earliest entries give his place of birth and state whether he is married or unmarried. Up to 1738, his age is usually given. After that date, the name of the notary's father is sometimes given, eg, 'Andrew Shand Writer in Thurso Son to Andrew Shand tennant at Innes in parish of Urquhart' was admitted as a notary public on 17 June 1742 (NP2/24).

21.5 The start of some lawyers' careers can be traced from the record of their apprenticeship, which may be found recorded in the register of deeds of their local sheriff court. By the late nineteenth century almost all the apprenticeships in these registers relate to legal practitioners rather than apprentices bound to masters involved in commerce or a trade.

22

Architects and Surveyors

22.1 If you are looking for an architect before 1840, first look at *A Biographical Dictionary of British Architects 1600-1840* by Howard Colvin (3rd edition, Yale University Press, 1995). For information about a Scottish architect of any date, look at *Scottish Architects' Papers: A Source Book* by Rebecca M Bailey (The Rutland Press, 1996). This gives NAS references for relevant material (under 'SRO' since the book predates the NAS name-change in

Vignette on plan showing name of surveyor, 1797 (RHP11610/1).

1999). You may also wish to contact the National Monuments Record of Scotland (address in Appendix A), who may provide you with relevant references in the NAS and elsewhere. In the NAS itself, there is a source list on Art and Architecture and a partial card index of references to architects in GD collections to consult. (There is a similar card index of artists.)

22.2 The profession of surveyor did not exist in Scotland until the mid-eighteenth century. For information about most surveyors before 1850, look at the *Dictionary of Land Surveyors and Local Map-Makers of Great Britain and Ireland, 1530-1850* by Sarah Bendall (1997) in two volumes. The entries in it are brief, but will show whether it may be worth your while to search further.

22.3 Information in the NAS about the plans and drawings produced by surveyors and architects is largely to be found in the Register House Plans (RHP). These plans are arranged and numbered in order of accession and there are now over 100,000 of them. Descriptions of non-architectural plans up to RHP4999 are contained in the *Descriptive List of Plans in the Scottish Record Office* volumes 1 to 4 (Scottish Record Office), which you should find in a library. Copies are also available for purchase from the National Archives of Scotland. Each volume is indexed. The full NAS plans catalogue is available on the NAS electronic catalogue, and it is possible to search this by place or by the name of an architect or surveyor.

∽ 23 ∽

Railwaymen

23.1 The NAS holds the surviving records of those railway companies that operated in Scotland. There used to be many railway companies which gradually amalgamated. Their records are listed, by railway company, in the BR catalogue. In the first volume of this catalogue, there is a list of the companies, giving the reference of each. For example, the records of the Glasgow and South-Western Railway Company are referenced BR/GSW. The catalogue is arranged in alphabetical order of reference letters. Within the records of each company, staff records are mostly listed in section 15. Thus, the staff records of the Highland Railway Company are referenced BR/HR/15. Some staff records may be found also in section 4 (miscellaneous records).

23.2 As a first step, if possible, look at a booklet compiled by Tom Richards, *Was Your Grandfather A Railwayman?* (Federation of Family History Societies), a directory of railway archive sources for family historians. This gives useful advice on how railway staff records were kept and lists briefly the railway staff records held by the NAS and other institutions.

23.3 Staff recorded in the railway records are those who worked for the railway companies, not those who built the lines and who worked for contractors. If your ancestor was a navvy, you are very unlikely to find a record of him as such. If your ancestor worked for a railway company, you are more likely to find a record of his service if he worked in a station than if he was an engine-driver or plate-layer. You are also more likely to find him if he worked for the North British Railway Company, because more of the NB's staff records have survived.

23.4 You have to know what railway company employed your ancestor. If you know where he lived, particularly if he lived in a rural area, you may be able to guess which company. If he lived in Dufftown, you may presume that he worked for the Great North of Scotland Railway Company. If he lived in Glasgow, it may be impossible to guess which company. To find the routes and stations of the pre-1923 railway companies, look at *British Railways: Pre-Grouping Atlas and Gazetteer* (Ian Allan Ltd). In the NAS, the Station Handbooks (BR/RCH(S)/5) also tell you which companies operated which stations.

23.5 There are various types of staff records and no great consistency in compiling them. The most useful staff registers are those which give the date of birth and show the detailed career of each railwayman, from job to job and place to place. For example, BR/CAL/15/1 shows that one John Anderson (born 15 January 1866) started work for the Caledonian Railway Company as a porter at Airth in 1881 and gradually advanced till he completed his career in 1924 as station-master at Guthrie on a salary of £260 per year. Other records will tell you who was employed in a particular station or department and why they ceased to be employed, either by a move to another station or department or by the end of their service. John Miller was employed by the Caledonian for 10 weeks in 1864 as a striker [metal-worker], before being discharged for smoking (BR/CAL/15/22). Offence books may tell you that your ancestor was drunk on duty

North British railwaymen, late nineteenth century (BR/NBR/4/315).
Reproduced by courtesy of BRB (Residuary) Limited.

or overslept and thereby delayed a train. Engine drivers were fined for not having steam up in time for their train's departure (eg in BR/GPK/4/1).

23.6 Staff records are a tiny part of the BR records but your ancestor is likely to be named in other records, such as minutes or correspondence, only if he was fairly high-up in the hierarchy or involved in an accident, eg 'David Renton, Platelayer, was run over and killed by an Engine on the Line' (1854-BR/EDP/1/5). The appointment of station masters and above are usually noted in directors' minutes (section 1), though often only the surname is given. If the minute book has an index, look under the name of the station.

23.7 Some railway records have survived in private collections, of which there are some in the GD series. These may include staff records. For instance GD422/1/89 is a Glasgow and South Western Railway Company staff register, 1874-1922. The staff recorded in it include women, particularly some employed during the 1914-1918 war. One was Mary Brown Auld, whose service as a parcel clerk was dispensed with in 1919 'owing to a male being engaged'.

$\mathcal{O}$ *24* $\mathcal{O}$

Coal Miners

24.1 Despite their historically low status, records of the names of colliers or coal miners can survive among the records of the landowner or coal company for whom they worked. In the NAS, such records are to be found among the GD collections and National Coal Board (later the British Coal Corporation) records (CB), which include records of coal companies before nationalisation. Look first at the Coal-mining source list, which will guide you to any relevant records. None will be indexed. The CB records are mainly twentieth century, but do include some eighteenth and nineteenth century records. In them, look for wages books, pay books, oncost books and output books: the names of workers appear in records of work done by them and of payments to them.

24.2 Because the colliers are usually described simply by forename and surname, care is required to ensure that you have found the right man, as is evidenced by a list of colliers at Edmonstone Colliery in 1777 (GD18/1124). The 39 colliers listed include three named Hugh Adam, three John Archibalds and several duplicated names.

24.3 Very occasionally you may find direct genealogical evidence. For example, the information 'Decr 1st 1753 Walter Simmer Son to old Thomas Simmer Entred Coliar' is noted in a Loanhead coal book in the Clerk of Penicuik muniments (GD18/990/7).

24.4 Among the Stirling Sheriff Court records, there are lists of colliers in Stirlingshire who in 1799 were in debt to the proprietors of their collieries (SC67/63/6). This is in accordance with a provision of the Colliers (Scotland) Act, 1799, which directed that debts due by colliers to their masters would cease to be valid unless they were recorded in sheriff court books within three months. There may, therefore, be such records in the records of other sheriff courts for that year.

24.5 If your ancestor met with an accident in a mine between 1861 and 1895, his name and that of the mine should be recorded in Procedure Books in the Lord Advocate's records (AD12/19-21). Mining accidents may also feature in the sheriff court fatal accident inquiries (7.31) and workmen's compensation series (13.43).

❧ 25 ❧

Trade and Business

Burgesses, Craftsmen and Apprentices

25.1 If your ancestor was engaged in trade or business in a royal burgh, then he should appear as a burgess in the records of that burgh and possibly as a member of the guild or incorporation of his particular craft in the records of that guild or incorporation. The record of his admission as a burgess or as a member or apprentice of his craft will sometimes state a relationship. Burgesses were usually the sons or sons-in-law of burgesses. An apprenticeship commenced with an agreement (known as an indenture) between the boy's father and his master. Craftsmen admitted would usually be the sons, sons-in-law or apprentices of members of the craft.

25.2 The Scottish Record Society has published alphabetical or indexed lists of the admissions of burgesses of Edinburgh, Canongate, Glasgow and Dumbarton and of apprentices of Edinburgh. The Dumfriesshire and Galloway Natural History and Antiquarian Society published its first Record Text in 1980, which included Dumfries burgesses from 1644 to the present. The Ayrshire Federation of Historical Societies has recently published a list of 'The burgesses and guild brethren of Ayr, 1647-1846'. For other burghs, you will have to search the available unindexed records. Look at the catalogue of burgh records (B) in the NAS to see if the records of your burgh include burgess rolls or court books, which will contain the admission of burgesses. You will hope to find entries such as 'John Broun pedlar, who married Elizabeth Mure Laufull daughter of the deceast James Mure burgess of this Burgh, in her pure Virginity…was…Admitted Burgess and freeman of the Burgh' (Dunbar, 22 July 1730, B18/32/7). Remember that many burgh records are not kept in the NAS but are held in the region where the burgh lies.

25.3 The NAS holds the records of the following crafts either among the burgh or Exchequer records or in the GD collections:

Baxters (bakers) of Haddington (B30/18/1).

Carters in Leith (GD399).

Cordiners (shoemakers) of the Canongate (GD1/14); Edinburgh (GD 348); Haddington (B30/18/2 and GD302/62-66 and 128-129); Selkirk (GD1/13).

Dyers or Litsters of Aberdeen (E870/4).

Fleshers (butchers) of Ayr (E870/6); Haddington (B30/18/3).

Goldsmiths of Edinburgh and Glasgow (GD1/482).

Hammermen (metal workers) of Burntisland (B9/13/2); Haddington (GD302/130-135); Linlithgow (GD76/390); Musselburgh (B52/8/4-6); Perth (GD1/427).

Tailors of Edinburgh (GD1/12); Linlithgow (GD76/385-391).

Weavers of Ayr (E870/5); Burntisland (B9/15); Haddington (B30/18/9).

Wrights and masons of Haddington (B30/18/4-8 and B30/22); Leith (GD1/943).

Wrights of Culross (GD1/977); Musselburgh (B52/8/1-3).

25.4 Some craft incorporation records kept elsewhere have been listed by the National Register of Archives for Scotland. Look in the index of NRAS surveys under the names of the burgh or in the classified index under 'Guilds and Incorporations'.

25.5 There are no such records of tradesmen who operated outwith the burghs. However, tradesmen and craftsmen may also be named in the records of mutual benefit societies associated with their trade and craft. The GD series include the records of the Society of Free Fishermen of Newhaven (GD265) and the Ancient Fraternity of Free Gardeners of East Lothian (GD420). The official series of friendly society records (FS) consist largely of rules and regulations of the societies. Only a very few include mid-nineteenth-century lists of members, eg the Strathaven Weavers Friendly Society (FS1/16/204). Such information is not noted in the FS catalogue but can be found in *Labour Records in Scotland* by Ian MacDougall (Scottish Labour History Society). Membership of such societies sometimes extended beyond those who were strictly of the stated trade.

25.6 Indentures of apprenticeship, whereby a boy became bound to serve a craftsman while he learned the craft, are noted in craft records. A few such indentures were registered in registers of deeds (see Chapter 12). Some survive in the GDs or similar collections, eg there is a series of indentures of Edinburgh apprentices referenced RH9/17/274-326. Some Edinburgh apprentices between 1695 and 1934 are recorded in the records of George Heriot's Trust (GD421, section 10). Do not expect an indenture to have survived: it is a bonus if it has done so.

25.7 From 1710, stamp duty was charged on indentures of apprenticeship. The collection of this tax was organised from London and no separate Scottish record seems to have been kept. Some Scottish apprentices are, however, recorded in the Stamp Board's Apprenticeship Books, 1710-1811, which are kept in The National Archives in London, reference IR1.

Business Records

25.8 Surviving business records may or may not include wages books or other records which name employees. There are some business records in the GD series. For example, those of the Carron Company (GD58) and of Alex Cowan & Son Ltd, papermakers in Penicuik, GD311, include staff records. Business books, including wages books, are also to be found among the Court of Session records (see Chapter 13). Look also in the National Register of Archives for Scotland catalogue and classified index for records of business firms.

Board of Manufactures

25.9 If your ancestor was involved in fabric manufacture or the fishing industry from 1727 into the nineteenth century, you might want to examine the records of the Board of Trustees for Fisheries, Manufactures and Improvements in Scotland, which was established to assist economic development. Look at the catalogue referenced NG1. Among its projects, the Board awarded premiums to producers and appointed stampmasters and other inspectors to supervise the linen industry. Thus, in 1792, there were awards of £25 to William Douglas at Dalhousie for his Silesia Linen and of £15 to Donald McLeod in Arnol Island of Lewis, for oil produced from dog fish (NG1/42/2); while, in 1822, we are told that Thomas Faulds was growing 'mostly promising' flax on the farm of Lissens in the parish of Dalry (NG1/42/8). The regulation of the linen industry was ended in 1823, but there are superannuation records of the former inspectors up to 1859, sometimes giving their age or date of death (NG1/48/1).

25.10 From 1809, the responsibility for overseeing the fishing industry passed to the Fishery Board for Scotland. The names of some of the men involved in the fishing industry occur in its records, particularly the records of the local fishery offices (AF17-36), but it may take some trawling to find a name you want. Among the surviving records of fishery vessels are a few registers of establishment for the fishery cruisers the *Brenda* and the *Minna*, which include information about place and date of birth and service records of the crew, c.1898-1954 (AF6/65-8).

Licensees

25.11 From 1756, a person who sold ale or other excisable liquors, whether in an inn or a shop, was required to have a licence. If he operated within a burgh, then the licence was granted by the burgh court, and, if outwith a burgh, by the Justices of the Peace for the county. Look in the B or JP catalogue at the contents list of the relevant burgh or county for the licensing court records. Some such records are kept in local archives. Most of the surviving records start in the nineteenth century. We find, for example, that Mrs Isabella Laing, shipbuilder, was licensed in 1829 to sell ale in a house at the Shore of Dunbar (B18/12/1).

༄ *26* ༄

Electors and Elected

Electors until 1832

26.1 Before 1832 only a tiny minority of Scotsmen (no women) elected representatives to Parliament, and the records of such elections are unlikely to add to the information you have about your ancestors. Representatives of the burghs were elected by the burgh council or by delegates of the councils: information is in the council minute books (B catalogue). Representatives of the counties were elected by freeholders, who were men who owned land or other heritable property in that county above a certain substantial value. The records of admission of landowners on to a roll of freeholders and of the election by the freeholders of a member of parliament are to be found among the sheriff court records. Look in the contents list of an appropriate SC catalogue to see if it contains the freeholders' records for that county. However, as, before a man was admitted to a roll of freeholders, the instrument of sasine which proved his ownership of sufficient land had to be recorded in the Register of Sasines (see 10.3-15), the freeholders records may add nothing to what you have already found in that register. There may be points of interest where the admission or vote of a freeholder was disputed by his political opponents.

Electors since 1832

26.2 Since 1832, various Reform Acts have gradually expanded the electorate. By 1929, almost everyone over 21 was on the electoral register. Until 1918, parliamentary electors had to be male and proprietors or tenants of lands, houses or other heritable property or (since 1868) prosperous lodgers. *Electoral Registers Since 1832* by Jeremy Gibson and Colin Rogers (Federation of Family History Societies), though written from an English point of view, is useful in describing the background of electoral law. Its list of Scottish records is incomplete.

Register of Voters in North Berwick

	N°	Date	Name	Calling
7 Sept 1839. Expunge	1	~~30 Aug 1838~~	~~Adam Moa Maxwell~~	Surgeon
	2	10 Sept 1833	Beshie George	Farmer
5 Sept 1840. Expunge	3	~~22 Sept 1832~~	~~Bertram Peter~~	Baker
	4	20 Aug 1838	Brash James [2]	Mason
	5	22 Sept 1838	Brodie James [3]	Baker
	6	"	Brown Rev° George [4]	Minister
Re-enrolled 7 Sept 1839	7	10 Sept 1833	Brown W™ Frederick Esq	Gentleman
	8	22 Sept 1832	Craven John [5]	Butler
	9	"	Craven William [9]	Farmer
	10	"	Crawford Alexander [10]	"
	11	8 Sept 1834	Crawford John	Mattster
	12	10 Sept 1833	Dall James [12]	Merchant
	13	6 Sept 1836	Dalrymple Sir New [13]	Gentleman
7 Sept 1839 Expunge	14	~~30 Aug 1838~~	~~Edington Peter~~	Grocer & Draper
	15	"	Eles George [17]	Flesher
	16	10 Sept 1833	Ferguson Robert Esq [18]	Gentleman
	17	22 Sept 1832	Graham Rob? R. V. [20]	Minister
	18	8 Sept 1835	Handyside Peter	Farmer
	19	10 Sept 1833	Herkes Alex [22]	Weaver
	20	"	Hislop James [23]	Shoemaker
	21	30 Aug 1838	Hood John [24]	Farmer
	22	22 Sept 1832	Kemp Thomas [25]	Baker
	23	30 Aug 1838	Low James [26]	Wright
	24	22 Sept 1832	Ramage George [29]	Farmer
Expunge 2 Sept 1852	25	30 Aug 1838	Ramage Henry	Baker
Re-enrolled 7 Sept 1839	26	"	Richardson Andrew	Tenant in Abbey
	27	9 Sept 1837	Sime George [32]	Parochial School Master
	28	22 Sept 1832	Smith George [33]	Carrier
	29	30 Aug 1838	Somerville James [34]	Clothy Merchant
	30	1st Sept 1838	...	...

Excerpt from Register of Voters in North Berwick, 1838.

26.3 Until 1918, electoral registers had to record why an elector had the right to vote. Thus, they provide not only the name of the voter, but also his occupation, whether he is a proprietor or tenant, and a description of his property.

26.4 From 1882, provided they were proprietors or tenants, unmarried women and married women not living in family with their husband could vote for burgh councillors and, from 1889, for county councillors. From these dates, there are supplementary registers of female voters for use in local government elections.

26.5 Registers of voters survive intermittently. Those in the NAS are almost entirely nineteenth–century, when burghs were in separate constituencies from the counties that surrounded them. Therefore there are separate registers of voters in burghs and counties, though some registers of burgh voters survive among sheriff court records. Most burghs were grouped together, so that several burghs (sometimes in different counties) were combined to form one constituency. County registers are arranged by parishes. There are the following registers of voters in the burgh and sheriff court records in the NAS. Check the relevant catalogue to obtain the exact reference.

> **Burghs:** Culross, 1832–1851 (B12/7). Dunbar, 1832–1860 (B18/18). Dunfermline, 1868 (SC67/61). Earlsferry, 1902–1904 (SC20/46). Falkirk, 1840–1865 (SC67/61). Hamilton, 1864–1865 (SC67/61). Lauder, 1832–1861 (B46/9). Newburgh, 1833–1870 (B54/9). Newport, 1899–1900 (SC20/46). North Berwick, 1832–1915 (B56/12). Perth, 1876–1877 and 1892–1893 (SC49/58). Stirling, 1868 (SC67/61).

> **Counties:** Caithness, 1832–1860 (SC14/64). Clackmannan and Kinross, 1832–1862 (SC64/63/26-36). Cromarty, 1832–1833 (SC24/21). Inverness, 1832–1872 (SC29/71). Kirkcudbright, 1832–1862 (SC16/68). Linlithgow, 1837 (SC41/99). Nairn, 1847–1873 (SC31/60). Peebles, 1832–1861 (SC42/44). Roxburgh, Hawick district, 1832–1846 (SC62/73). Selkirk, 1832–1861 (SC63/61). Stirling, 1832–1862 (SC67/61). Wigtown, 1832–1861 (SC19/64).

26.6 Some of these sheriff court records also include poll books and other records of voters. Similar records may occasionally be found in GD collections, most notably GD260, which includes electoral registers for the county of Dumbarton, 1873–1892 (GD260/4/1-5). Enquiries about records of voters should also be made to local archives and libraries.

Members of Parliament

26.7 Though the records described above will sometimes mention those elected, you should use printed sources if you are searching for an ancestor who might have been a representative in Parliament. These include the following:

> *The Parliaments of Scotland: Burgh and Shire Commissioners,* edited by Margaret D Young (Scottish Academic Press, 1992-3) contains some 2,000 brief biographies, arranged in alphabetical order, of the men who represented the burghs and counties in the Scottish Parliament until 1707. It also contains an appendix, listing the constituencies alphabetically with names of the representatives of each.
>
> *Members of Parliament, Scotland, 1357-1882* by Joseph Foster.
>
> *The History of Parliament. The House of Commons.* A series of volumes covering 1690-1820 (History of Parliament Trust).
>
> *Who's Who of British Members of Parliament, 1832-1979* (The Harvester Press).

🏵 27 🏵

The Sick and Insane

The Sick

27.1 Records of patients in hospitals often supply the patient's age and some-times date of death. Hospital records are largely in the custody of the archivist of the Health Board within whose authority the hospital lies (see addresses in Appendix A). Such records formerly in the NAS have been transmitted to the relevant Health Boards, except for a series of registers of out-patients of Dundee Royal Infirmary, 1851-1854, (CS96/2279-2304) and the records of the Kelso Dispensary and Cottage Hospital (HH71). The Kelso records include lists of patients in the hospital, since 1777, supplying the patient's name, parish, age, date of admission, disease and the outcome (mostly 'cured'). Thus, we learn that Margaret Cummins, resident in the parish of Eccles, aged 60, poisoned with laudanum, was admitted on 10 January 1828, was treated but died (HH71/44). There are also some records of out-patients and patients visited at home.

27.2 Those prevented by illness from earning a living might have received poor relief (see 28.1-11). For example, in 1727, the parish of Inveravon supported 'John Fleeming a poor boy lyable to an epilepsie' (CH2/191/2, p244).

'Lunatics'

27.3 The words 'lunatic' and 'insane' are used here to describe people suffering various grades of mental disturbance, which were sometimes not fully understood at the time. Records may survive if someone was appointed to administer the property of an insane person, or if he were put in the custody of an asylum or individual.

27.4 Obviously, only when the insane person owned property was there a need to go to law to decide who should be curator to administer that property. Until 1897, such decisions might be 'retoured to Chancery' in the same procedure as heirs were proved. This is explained in 9.4-22. Up to 1700, these decisions are to be found in the 'Inquisitiones de Tutela' in volume 2 of the *Inquisitionum Retornatarum Abbreviatio* (indexed in volume 3). After 1700, look in the 'Index to Tutories and Curatories in Record of Retours, 1701-1897'. The people indexed in this include insane persons, identifiable by being given a curator, not a tutor. To see the retour, order out by C22 and the volume number given in the index. The curator was usually the nearest male relative on the father's side aged at least 25 years.

27.5 The retour will tell you which sheriff court held the preceding inquiry. Where records of these inquiries survive, they may provide more details both of the condition of the insane person and of his relationship to his curator. Look in the relevant SC catalogue for 'Record of Services' or similar heading. For example, in 1830, James Mitchell, teacher, Kineff, was appointed curator to administer the affairs of William Gordon, bookseller, Aberdeen, his maternal uncle (C22/133, f.89). The related Aberdeen Sheriff Court records (SC1/27/20) supply the date of James's baptism and the names of his parents and William's father.

27.6 In the eighteenth century, an alternative procedure developed whereby a near relative petitioned the Court of Session for the judicial appointment of a 'curator bonis' to look after the affairs of an insane or otherwise incapable person. The records of such cases are among the records of the Court of Session (see 13.3 onwards).

27.7 After 1880, when the estate of an incapable person did not exceed £100 in yearly value, the appointment of a curator bonis could also be made by a sheriff court. A few sheriff courts kept a separate record of these appointments (perhaps in a 'Register of Judicial Factors'), but mostly they have to be sought among the ordinary court records (see 13.38-42).

27.8 From 1849, the Accountant of Court (of Session) was responsible for supervising curators appointed to administer the estates of persons unable to administer their own affairs. Therefore, the Accountant of Court's records include information about better-off lunatics, including cases where the curator bonis had been appointed before 1849. Look at CS313-317 in the Court of Session catalogue.

27.9 Many patients, of all social grades but the majority paupers, were kept in asylums. There are few records of such asylums prior to 1858. Among the Aberdeen Sheriff Court records, there are registers of lunatics in asylums in Aberdeenshire between 1800 and 1823 and between 1855 and 1857 (SC1/18/1-2).

27.10 A statutory licensing and inspection system was established for all public and private institutions in Scotland having 'the care or confinement of furious and fatuous persons and lunatics'. Inspection reports were submitted to the Royal College of Physicians in Edinburgh and the High Court of Justiciary. Within the JC records there have survived reports, accounts and returns on madhouses and lunatics, 1816-1857 (JC54). The reports (especially the early ones) contain detailed medical and social comment on named patients in public and private asylums and private houses, and observations on buildings and staff. In 1854 special reports were compiled giving the names and costs of maintaining lunatic paupers in each parish in Scotland for the years 1851-1853 (JC54/13-41).

27.11 From 1857, such asylums were regulated by the General Board of Commissioners in Lunacy. The Board's records are preserved in the NAS, listed in the Mental Welfare Commission (MC) catalogue, but are closed for 75 years. Their records include a general register of all lunatics in asylums (MC7). This lists and numbers the inmates chronologically, from number 1, Jean Morris, who was admitted to Newbigging House in 1805 (where she died 60 years later) to number 218,009 in 1962. Though this register apparently starts in 1805, it only records those who were still alive in 1858 or were committed since 1858. The register records name, date of admission, which asylum, date of death or discharge, and whither removed (if relevant). A partial index to the register is found at MC7/33: MC7/33/1 covers the period 1805-1962, letters O-Z only, and MC7/33/2 covers the period 1910-1955, letters A-G only. If the individual you are looking for falls outside either of these indexes, you will need to look through the registers or the Notices of Admission (see 27.12) themselves, and it therefore helps if you have an idea of when he might have been committed to an asylum.

27.12 Fuller details about those admitted to asylums since 1858 are contained in the Notices of Admission (MC2), which are arranged chronologically. The patient's number in the general register (MC7) is noted on his notice of admission. Information supplied, as well as their mental and physical health, includes full name, age, marital status, previous place of abode, nearest relative, and whether any member of his family had been insane.

We find that Robert Primrose Paterson, aged 29, single, schoolmaster at Duddingstone, whose insanity was supposedly caused by 'Studying Some Educational Scheme', was admitted to the Royal Edinburgh Asylum on the petition of his mother in January 1858 (MC2/1).

27.13 There is no register of lunatics who were not put into asylums, though they may be named in the records of poor relief (see Chapter 28). However, in the Lord Advocate's papers, there is a 'Return of lunatics or idiots at large in the county of Edinburgh (Midlothian)' in 1850 (AD58/114). This provides the name and age of each patient, with whom he resides and by whom supported.

27.14 Some people accused of a crime were found to be insane. Court records, particularly the High Court of Justiciary (JC), will record that a person was 'Insane in bar of trial' and committed to prison. These persons are recorded in the Justiciary trials catalogue. The Home and Health Department records include casebooks, dating from 1846, and later files on criminal lunatics (HH17, 18 and 21/48). These are closed for 75 years.

28

The Poor

28.1 The poor are always with us and provision has to be made for them. Records relating to their maintenance can be valuable sources of information for the genealogist whose ancestors were paupers for all or part of their lives. Until recently the problematical nature of these sources has deterred the majority of genealogists. However, the advent of large indexing projects run by some local authority archives and family history societies has opened up poor relief records to thousands of researchers.

28.2 Before searching for pauper ancestors, the researcher should first grasp three aspects of poor relief in Scotland before the mid-twentieth century: there was a distinction made between 'deserving' and 'undeserving' poor; until the 1930s relief was largely organised by parish; and record-keeping was particularly concerned with a pauper's parish of birth or settlement.

28.3 From the sixteenth century until the Great Depression of the 1920s, able-bodied men and women were regarded as undeserving recipients of poor relief. Acts of parliament regulating the provision of poor relief repeatedly reserved the provision of relief to the deserving poor; in effect those who lacked funds or family support and who were unable, through age or infirmity, to maintain themselves. These included the elderly who lived without family support, the disabled and insane, orphans and destitute children, and the mothers of young children deserted by their husbands. The able-bodied unemployed were not entitled to relief, but were sometimes given relief if injury or illness temporarily prevented them supporting their family. So much the acts allowed, but in practice parishes often gave help to vagrant poor, usually unnamed in the records – 'a stranger', 'a poor man at the church door'.

28.4 Each parish was bound to support the deserving poor living within its boundaries, provided they had either been born there or had acquired settlement there. Settlement could be acquired by residing in a parish for seven years or, in the case of married women, by adopting their husband's parish of birth or residence. The onus on each parish to ascertain whether someone claiming relief was entitled to it and was legally settled in the parish, meant that parishes might investigate the circumstances of the claimant's family and his or her movements from one residence to another over several years.

28.5 An important date in the provision of poor relief is 1845, when what is often termed the 'New Poor Law' was introduced. However, for genealogical purposes it is best to consider poor relief records as belonging to three periods: the late seventeenth century until the 1820s, the 1820s until the 1880s and the 1880s until 1930. From 1930 onwards poor relief was no longer managed by parishes and surviving poor relief records from that era onwards will almost certainly be closed to public access, due to the sensitive nature of the information about individual claimants.

Poor relief records from the 1690s until the 1820s

28.6 Before the Poor Law Act, 1845, the responsibility for poor relief lay jointly with the heritors (see 10.41) and kirk session of each parish, and records of payments to the poor may be found in the records of either (see 28.10-13 below). Burgh councils also made charitable payments to people in distress, but the burgh records (B) in the NAS are not very informative on this score, and searching through burgh minutes and accounts will, in general, be very time-consuming and unrewarding. Where local authority archives and libraries hold burgh records it may be worth enquiring whether local societies have carried out indexing.

Poor relief records from the 1820s until the 1880s

28.7 The Poor Law Act, 1845 set up parochial boards in Scotland's 878 parishes, and allowed them to fund poor relief from local property taxation rather than on church collections and contributions from heritors. The resultant transition from church authorities to what are termed 'civil parishes' took several decades. Only 230 parishes adopted the New Poor Law in 1845, but by 1865 only about 100 were still maintaining their poor as before. By the time parochial boards were replaced by parish councils in 1892 all Scotland's parishes operated under the same system.

28.8 In some parishes the parochial board continued to use the record-keeping practices of the heritors or kirk sessions, especially where registers of the poor had been compiled from the 1830s. After 1865 there was considerable standardisation in record keeping and registers compiled from then onwards often have information about paupers dating back to 1845 or earlier. Because of the overlap of responsibilities of kirk sessions, heritors and parochial boards, anyone searching for information about pauper ancestors in this transition period, therefore, should consult the records of kirk sessions and heritors (see 28.10-13 below), and the records of parochial boards (see 28.14-20 below).

Poor relief records from the 1880s until the 1930s

28.9 From the 1880s onwards you can be fairly certain that any surviving records relating to poor relief will be among civil parish records, which in most cases will be with local authority archives (see 28.14-20 below).

Poor relief catalogues in kirk session and heritors' records

28.10 Look in the indexes of parishes in both HR and CH2 repertories and then the relevant list of records for the particular parish. Some kirk session records are held under charge and superintendence by local authority archives, but most are held by the NAS. Almost all heritors' records are held by the NAS, but a few are held by local authority archives, often because these have begun life as heritors' minutes and become parochial board minutes. Poor relief accounts were occasionally kept as a separate record and as such will be specified in the HR or CH2 catalogue. For example, the heritors of Tranent kept a very detailed poor roll between 1827 and 1845, giving details such as '79, infirm, son silly' and, of a widow, '33, young children' (HR74/15/3). Much more commonly, payments to the poor are noted, in the midst of other business, in the minute books and account books kept by the heritors and kirk sessions. There is no shortcut to searching them, except in the few cases where the records have been indexed and/or published.

28.11 Income paid to the poor came from assessments on the heritors and collections at the church services. This 'poor money' was distributed to the 'Ordinary Poor' or 'Pensioners', who were paid at regular intervals and often appear in a list, and the 'Occasional Poor'. The latter category included payments in kind, such as supplying shoes or coal to a needy person; payments to the temporarily disabled, eg 10 shillings 'to one James Simpson who had his thigh bone broken' (Glencorse Kirk Session, 17 October 1700 – CH2/181/1); and payments to those who did not belong to the parish.

28.12 For the first decade after 1845 most kirk sessions and heritors continued for a time to provide for their poor from church collections and recorded payments in their minutes and accounts, eg Greenlaw kirk session distributed to named poor after the communion service twice yearly until 1881 (CH2/183/2). However, from the 1820s onwards the compilation of separate poor relief records became more common, and the information recorded therein more informative. The Dirleton heritors kept a roll of poor from 1825 until 1847 (HR42/4).

28.13 Though all infirm poor within the parish, whatever their denomination, were the responsibility of the established kirk session, the free churches also sometimes assisted their own poor. However, the names of their poor people are only occasionally reported in their records (CH3 and CH10-16).

Civil Parish Records

28.14 From 1845 onwards parochial boards kept minute books and accounts, but some boards also compiled more comprehensive registers of information on paupers. In 1865 record-keeping was standardised to a great extent by the body which supervised civil parishes at that time, the Board of Supervision, and from then on most parishes kept distinct types of registers (see 28.17-18 below). The records of parochial boards and parish councils are mainly held by local authority archives and libraries, but the NAS holds the records for 18 civil parishes in Wigtownshire (CO4/30-47), 24 civil parishes in East Lothian (CO7/7, DC4/4-11, DC5/4-5, and DC7/4) and 18 civil parishes in Midlothian (CO2/77-91). The Wigtownshire and East Lothian parish records contain minute books of parochial boards and parish councils, and registers of the poor. For the Midlothian parishes only minute books survive. In addition two volumes survive for the parishes of Forgan and Falkland in the County of Fife: a minute book for Forgan Parish Council, 1917-1929 (CO12/2) and the letter book of Falkland Parish's Inspector of the Poor, 1848-9 (CO12/1). Eventually all of these civil parish records are likely to be moved to appropriate local archives.

28.15 Minute books and accounts of parochial boards and parish councils contain information on applications for poor relief, but the amount of information depends on the parish. Some parishes merely recorded the names of successful applicants and the amount or type of relief. Other parishes recorded more details of individual applicants, but in most minute books

A page from a general register of the poor for Glasserton parish, Wigtownshire, 1865 (CO4/30/7).

the information may only confirm what the researcher already knows, or else add nothing of substance. In some cases a parochial board minute book might begin life as the minute book of the heritors and contain information on poor relief back to the 1830s. As with all minute books and accounts, they will require time-consuming research, unless they have been indexed. Very few are indexed. The researcher should only turn to the minute books of a parochial board or parish council when no separate registers of the poor survive for that parish (see 28.16–19 below).

Registers of the poor

28.16 From the 1840s (and in some cases the 1830s) many parishes began compiling registers of the poor giving full details of the people who were aided. These records are particularly useful in recording the children of aged paupers and the parentage of orphans and illegitimate and deserted children. They can also be useful in showing the geographical movements of an individual. Each parochial board had to keep a roll of poor persons to whom it gave financial relief. Among the information recorded about each pauper was age, country and place of birth, whether married or single, name and age of wife and children living with the pauper, and name and age of husband or wife and children not living in family with the pauper. Thus, we find from the register of poor of Inch parish in Wigtownshire, that Sarah Ann Hawthorne or Caldwell, a washerwoman, who declined to go into the poorhouse in 1891, was 72, born in Ireland, and had 9 children, 5 of whom were in America (CO4/32/7, p408).

28.17 In 1865 the Board of Supervision imposed a greater degree of standardisation on record-keeping by parochial boards. From then on most parishes compiled what was known as a 'General Register of the Poor', which was in effect a record of successful applicants for relief. In some cases information about paupers on the parishes' books since the 1830s was included and researchers should be careful when considering the ages of individuals recorded, as these may be the ages in 1865, not at the time of the original application many years earlier. Likewise it is important to note that the information was added to these registers over time, but in most cases this is quite clear from the dating of the entries and the changes in handwriting. Note that the term 'General Register of the Poor' does not mean that a central register was kept for the whole of Scotland. General registers were kept by individual parishes and their name differentiates them from other types of registers, such as children's separate registers (also introduced in 1865) and registers of able-bodied unemployed (introduced in the 1920s, when poor relief was extended to include workers made unemployed during the Great Depression).

28.18 Not everyone who applied for poor relief was added to the poor roll. Some information about failed applicants and those who were not added to the roll of regular poor may be found in parochial board/civil parish minutes. In 1852, the parochial board of Inch 'took up the case of Mrs Jean Finlay. The Board agree to pay the passage of her four children from Liverpool to America' (CO4/32/1), although there was no provision in the Poor Law (Scotland) Act for assisting emigration. From 1865 most parishes kept registers of applications for relief (some parishes had been keeping similar registers from the 1850s or even earlier). The value of such registers is that they contain information about all applicants for relief, not merely the successful ones whose details can be found in general registers etc.

28.19 Apart from the records for civil parishes in Wigtownshire, East Lothian, Midlothian and Fife held by the NAS (see 28.14 above), most civil parish records are held by local authority archives and libraries. In many cases only minute books and accounts survive. In the case of the four largest cities, substantial runs of poor relief registers apparently survive for Glasgow only (held by Glasgow City Archives). For the rest of Scotland the survival of registers of the poor is variable. Substantial sets of poor registers are held by Shetland Council Archives (Shetland), Orkney Council Archives (Orkney), the North Highland Archive at Wick (Caithness), Highland Council Archive (Sutherland, Ross & Cromarty, Inverness-shire, Inverness Burgh), Aberdeen City Archives (Aberdeenshire), Angus Council Archives (Angus), Dundee City Archives (one parish in Angus), Glasgow City Archives (Glasgow City, Lanarkshire, Renfrewshire, Dunbartonshire), Renfrew Council Libraries in Paisley (Paisley Burgh), Ayrshire Archives (Ayrshire), and Dumfries & Galloway Libraries (Dumfriesshire and Kirkcudbrightshire). The Scottish Archive Network (*www.scan.org.uk*) can provide information about the location of most of these. There appear to be major gaps for several counties: most notably for parishes in Fife and Perthshire.

Indexing projects

28.20 Access to poor relief registers for certain areas of Scotland has been greatly increased by large scale indexing projects carried out by archives and family history societies. The largest of these is the database index at Glasgow City Archives to poor relief registers compiled by parishes in Glasgow, Lanarkshire, Renfrewshire, Lanarkshire and Dunbartonshire. Indexing has also been carried out on some poor registers in Ayrshire by the East Ayrshire Family History Society, and on registers for some parishes in Aberdeenshire by the Aberdeen & North East of Scotland Family History Society. At the time of writing none of these is available online and enquiries should be directed to the archive or society concerned. One index of poor relief records which is online is a combined index to Liff & Benvie Parochial Board's Register of Poor (1854-1865) and Dundee East Poorhouse Register (1856-1878), compiled by Friends of Dundee City Archives and accessible at *http://www.fdca.org.uk/*.

Poor relief records in court records

28.21 An applicant who was refused relief by the inspector of poor for a parish could appeal to the sheriff of the sheriffdom in which that parish lay. An inspector of poor could apply to the sheriff for the removal from the country of a pauper who was not a native of Scotland, and also could raise an action in the sheriff court against a father who had deserted his wife and children or refused to support an illegitimate child. The sheriff court records (SC) therefore contain records of such cases.

28.22 A few sheriff courts kept separate records relating to poor relief appeals and related matters, but most of these cover only a limited period, such as the 'poor law minute books' compiled by Ayr Sheriff Court for 1846-1862 (SC6/82). These give the name of the appellant, the parish, and the date and decision of the case. In most cases, the records of appeal cases relating to poor relief have to be sought among the records of other Ordinary Court cases brought before the sheriff (see 13.38-42). Identifying them may not be easy and the detail given may be minimal. If there is a register of summary applications, look there. Glasgow Sheriff Court's register (SC36/7) is particularly useful, as it starts in 1858, earlier than most. In such a register, look under 'Pursuer or Applicant' for a person appealing against refusal of relief and under 'Respondent' for a person who was to be removed to Ireland or England or had deserted wife and children.

28.23 For those whose ancestor appealed to a sheriff court after an unfavourable decision by a civil parish, a potential shortcut to information exists in the form of two published works. The first of these is Alexander McNeel Caird's *Poor Law Manual for Scotland*, published in Edinburgh in at least six editions between 1845 and 1851. In addition to summarising the statutes relating to the relief of the poor, Caird provides a digest of over 60 selected cases relating to poor law in sheriff courts, the Court of Session and the High Court of Justiciary. For the period after 1851 anyone researching poor relief appeals should consult the *Poor Law Magazine*, which published a monthly digest of appeal cases. An edition of Caird is available in the West Search Room (library reference W243) and digital copies of the pages in Caird relating to appeal cases are available in the Historical Search Room. Bound copies of the *Poor Law Magazine* are widely available in Scottish archives and reference libraries.

Destitution

28.24 The parish system of poor relief sometimes proved insufficient and had to be supplemented by private charity. To find the records of charitable foundations, sometimes called 'hospitals', which helped the poor of particular localities, you should first check the regional or district archive which serves that locality. The records of the King James VI Hospital, Perth, are in the NAS. Look in the GD79 inventory at section 7 for records of the deserving poor of Perth. In 1825, an application was made on behalf of the Widow Macphail, in South Street, aged 102 years (GD79/7/38/1).

28.25 In the cities, charitable institutions were established for the maintenance and education of orphans and other destitute children. Two such institutions whose records are held by the NAS are the Dean Orphanage (GD417)

Children at the Orphan Hospital of Edinburgh, later the Dean Orphanage, eighteenth century (GD417/255/9). Reproduced by courtesy of the Secretaries and Treasurers of the Dean Orphanage and Cauvin's Trust.

and Dr Guthrie's Schools (GD425), both in Edinburgh. Records which name children date from 1753 and 1854 respectively, but these records less than 100 years old are closed to the public. Petitions for admission and admission registers can provide useful family information. James Ralston, admitted to Dean Orphanage in 1830, was the son of an army sergeant. His mother 'also followed the Camp since she was 11 years of age', suffering fatigue and exposure during the Peninsular Campaigns (GD417/175).

28.26 In response to the devastating failure of the potato crop in 1846, destitution boards were established to raise money to save the people of the Highlands and Islands from starvation. The records of these boards, listed in the Highland Destitution (HD) catalogue, name many of the people in the Highlands and Islands who between 1847 and 1852 were given meal or financial aid or were found work. Look at the registers listed as HD1. These registers vary in content but usually supply the name, age and occupation of each head of family, sometimes also the number of children in that family, and sometimes the names and ages of everyone in the family. Thus, we find that in May 1847, Mathew Jameson, a farmer and fisherman at Ollabury in the district of Northmaven in Shetland, was 35 and had one child above 12 and four under 12 (HD1/1). A register of the most needy families in Skye in 1850 (HD1/13) tells us that Donald McDiarmid, at Kilmuir in the district of Watternish, was aged 60 and his family consisted of Alice (45), Norman (7) and John (4). HD1 is not a complete series, but similar information can be found in meal distribution accounts (HD6/9-13) and in some of the papers relating to Shetland (HD17), Skye (HD20) and Wester Ross (HD21), particularly the abstracts of registry and applications for work. An equivalent record in the Tobermory Sheriff Court records is a register of meal distribution, 1848-1853, to paupers in and around Mull (SC59/15/5).

28.27 For a fuller summary of poor relief records in the NAS see Kirsty M Forbes and Robert H J Urquhart, 'Records in the National Archives of Scotland relating to Poor Relief, 1845-1930' in *Scottish Archives* volume 8 (2002).

29

Emigrants and Migrants

29.1 There is ample proof that Scotsmen migrated, both within the British Isles and overseas. Yet records of the actual movement of individual migrants are sparse. Most people searching for emigrant ancestors assume they will appear in a ship's passenger list: sadly this is not the case (see 3.21 for possible sources). Official ship passenger lists exist only from 1890 and these are held in The National Archives in London. Free movement within the United Kingdom has always been possible, but the evidence has to be dug out of records designed for other purposes, such as kirk session or parochial board records. There is no official record of the ordinary Scots who migrated to Northern Ireland in the reign of James VI, only of their well-to-do landlords.

29.2 There was similar freedom of travel abroad, generally unrecorded except for transported criminals (see 14.23). Passports, as we know them, were not introduced until 1915. Previously, the Crown sometimes issued passes or letters of protection to people travelling in Europe, but these people were from the upper classes and intending to return. Before 1603, some of these letters were recorded in the Register of the Privy Seal (see 7.17). Records of later passports are mainly in The National Archives in London.

29.3 If your ancestor emigrated to North America or Australia, look for him in the immigration records in the country of arrival or in the various published lists which are available such as:

> *Passenger and Immigration Lists Index – A Guide to Published Arrival Records of about 500,000 Passengers in the United States and Canada* by P William Filby and Mary K Meyer (Gale Research Company, Detroit).

> *Directory of Scottish Settlers in North America,* 1625-1825, 6 volumes, by David Dobson (Genealogical Publishing Company, Baltimore).

A Dictionary of Scottish Emigrants to the USA, 2 volumes, by Donald Whyte (Magna Carta Book Company, Baltimore).

A Dictionary of Scottish Emigrants to Canada Before Confederation by Donald Whyte (Ontario Genealogical Society).

29.4 There are, however, two bodies of records in the NAS that deal specifically with short-lived nineteenth century schemes to assist emigrants from the western Highlands and Islands.

29.5 The Highland and Island Emigration Society was a voluntary association formed in 1851 to assist those affected by the potato famine. Its records are referenced HD4. They include lists of assisted emigrants who sailed to Australia between 1852 and 1857 (HD4/5). The emigrants are listed by ship and by family, giving the name and age of each person and where they had resided in western Scotland. An index of the names of these emigrants is available online at *www.scan.org.uk/researchrtools/emigration.htm*.

29.6 Files concerning a later scheme for state-aided emigration to Canada are listed in the AF catalogue under AF51. Files which provide family details of those who applied to emigrate are dated between 1886 and 1889. They include lists of applicants from some of the Western Isles and completed forms of application for assistance to emigrate. These record the members of the household of the applicant, stating each's age and relationship to the applicant. If any failed to embark, this is noted. Thus, we know that William Macleod (26), from Coll, emigrated with his wife and brother, but his cousin Donald MacDonald changed his mind and stayed behind (AF51/36). Some information about emigrants in Manitoba after 1889 is contained in the records of the Crofters and Cottars Colonization Board (AF51/188-211).

❧ *30* ❧

Genealogies

30.1 If you have been through even some of the records covered in this book, you will want to draw up your own family tree. Unless you are of the aristocracy or landed gentry, you are not likely find your own family tree ready-made. However, there is a chance that you might link your family tree to one already compiled. Published genealogies of Scottish families are listed in *Scottish Family History* by Margaret Stuart and Balfour Paul and *Scottish Family Histories* by J P S Ferguson. Manuscript genealogies of varying antiquity may be found in archives and libraries, such as those of the Scottish Genealogy Society and the Lyon Office (addresses in Appendix A).

30.2 Be aware that not every genealogy may be totally accurate. Check the details if you can.

30.3 There are some genealogies among the manuscripts in the NAS. RH16 is a collection of genealogies, indexed at the end of the RH16 inventory. Otherwise, seek for genealogies in the GD collections. A few of the GDs consist of papers gathered and compiled by people who did research. From our point of view, the most useful of these is the John MacGregor Collection (GD50), which, along with original papers and transcripts of documents, contains genealogies and genealogical notes, mainly of Highland families, especially MacGregors and Campbells. As the GD50 inventory is arranged in no logical order, you should examine it carefully. Some GD collections of the records of landed and noble families include genealogies and family narratives, usually but not exclusively of their own and related families. These genealogies may or may not be evident in the inventory contents list: try the miscellaneous section, if there is one.

30.4 You will no doubt have realised by now that family history research is an absorbing and potentially endless pursuit. Having started out with the intention of researching their family history, many people embark on related research, such as the local history of the area in which their ancestors lived. If you wish to do this, you may find our companion guide *Tracing Scottish Local History* of value.

30.5 Let us take as our final words on the ancestors we seek an observation by the American writer Oliver Wendell Holmes: 'Every man is an omnibus in which his ancestors ride.' In tracing your family history, you may discover more about yourself.

∽ *Appendix A* ∽
Useful Addresses

National Institutions

National Archives of Scotland
HM General Register House
Edinburgh
EH1 3YY
Phone: 0131 535 1314
Fax: 0131 535 1360
www.nas.gov.uk

National Register of Archives for
   Scotland
West Register House
Charlotte Square
Edinburgh
EH2 4DF
Phone: 0131 535 1403
Fax: 0131 434 1311
www.nas.gov.uk/the_collections.htm

General Register Office for Scotland
New Register House
Edinburgh
EH1 3YT
Phone: 0131 334 0380
Fax: 0131 314 4400
www.gro-scotland.gov.uk

Court of the Lord Lyon
New Register House
Edinburgh
EH1 3YT
Phone: 0131 556 7255
Fax: 0131 557 2148

National Library of Scotland
George IV Bridge
Edinburgh
EH1 1EW
Phone: 0131 226 4531
Fax: 0131 226 4803
www.nls.uk

National Monuments Record of
   Scotland
Royal Commission on the Ancient and
   Historical Monuments of Scotland
16 Bernard Terrace
Edinburgh EH8 9NX
Phone: 0131 662 1456
Fax: 0131 662 1499
www.rcahms.gov.uk

The National War Museum of Scotland
Edinburgh Castle
Edinburgh
EHI 2NG
Phone: 0131 225 7534
Fax: 0131 225 3848
www.nms.ac.uk/war

Scottish Catholic Archives
16 Drummond Place
Edinburgh
EH3 6PL
Phone: 0131 556 3661

Scottish Jewish Archives Centre
129 Hill Street
Glasgow
G3 6UB
Phone: 0141 332 4911
www.sjac.org.uk

Family Records Centre
1 Myddelton Street
Islington
London
EC1R 1UW
Phone: 020 8392 5300
www.familyrecords.gov.uk/frc

The National Archives
Kew
Richmond
Surrey
TW9 4DU
Phone: 020 8876 3444
Fax: 020 8392 5286
www.nationalarchives.gov.uk

Public Record Office of Northern
Ireland
66 Balmoral Avenue
Belfast
BT9 6NY
Phone: (+44) 028 9025 5800
www.proni.nics.gov.uk

The National Archives of Ireland
Bishop Street
Dublin 8
Republic of Ireland
Phone: + 353 (1) 407-2300
Fax + 353 (1) 407-2333
www.nationalarchives.ie

Local Archives

Aberdeen Council Archives
Old Aberdeen House
Dunbar Street
Aberdeen
AB22 8YP
Phone: 01224 481775
Fax: 01224 495830
www.aberdeenshire.gov.uk

Aberdeen City Archives
Town House
Broad Street
Aberdeen
AB9 1AQ
Phone: 01224 522521
Fax: 01224 638556
*www.aberdeencity.gov.uk/acc_data/informa-
tion/arc_main.asp*

Angus Archives
Montrose Library
214 High Street
Montrose
DD10 8PH
Phone: 01674 671 415
Fax: 01674 671 810
www.angus.gov.uk/history/default.htm

Argyll and Bute Council Archives
Manse Brae
Lochgilphead
Argyll
PA31 8QU
Phone: 01546 604120
Fax: 01546 606897
www.argyll-bute.gov.uk

Ayrshire Archives
Ayrshire Archives Centre
Craigie Estate
Ayr
KA8 0SS
Phone: 01292 287 584
Fax: 01292 284 918
www.south-ayrshire.gov.uk/archives/

Clackmannanshire Council Archives
26-28 Drysdale Street
Alloa
FK10 1JL
Phone: 01259 722 262
Fax: 01259 219 469
www.clacksweb.org.uk/dyna/archives

Dumfries and Galloway Archives
Archive Centre
33 Burns Street
Dumfries
DG1 2PS
Phone: 01387 269254
Fax: 01387 264126
www.dumgal.gov.uk/services/depts/comres/
library/archives.htm

Dundee City Archives Support Services
21 City Square
Dundee
DD1 3BY
(Callers please use 1 Shore Terrace,
  Dundee)
Phone: 01382 434494
Fax: 01382 434666
www.dundeecity.gov.uk/archives

East Dunbartonshire Information and
  Archives
William Patrick Library
2 West High Street
Kirkintilloch
G66 1HW
Phone: 0141 776 8090
Fax: 0141 776 0408

Edinburgh City Archives
City Chambers
High Street
Edinburgh
EH1 1YJ
Phone: 0131 529 4616
Fax: 0131 529 4957
www.edinburgh.gov.uk

Edinburgh Room
Edinburgh City Libraries
Central Library
George IV Bridge
Edinburgh
EHI IEG
Phone: 0131 225 5584
www.edinburgh.gov.uk/libraries

Falkirk Council Archives
Falkirk Museums History Research
  Centre
Callendar House
Callendar Park
Falkirk FK1 1YR
Phone: 01324 503778
Fax: 01324 503771
www.falkirkmuseums.demon.co.uk

Fife Council Archive Centre
Carleton House
Balgonie Road
Markinch
KY7 6AQ
Phone: 01592 413256
Fax: 01592 417477

Glasgow City Archives and Special
  Collections
Mitchell Library
North Street
Glasgow
G3 7DN
Phone: 0141 287 2910
Fax: 0141 286 8452
www.glasgowlibraries.org

Highland Council Archive
Inverness Library
Farraline Park
Inverness
IV1 1LS
Phone: 01463 220 330
Fax: 01463 711 128
www.highland.gov.uk/educ/publicservices/
*   archivedetails/highlandarchive.htm*

Midlothian Council Archives
Library Headquarters
2 Clerk Street
Loanhead
EH20 9DR
Phone: 0131 271 3976
Fax: 0131 440 4635

Moray Council Local Heritage Centre
Grant Lodge
Cooper Park
Elgin
Moray
IV30 1HS
Phone: 01343 563413
Fax: 01343 549050
www.moray.org/heritage/index.html

North Highland Archive
Wick Library
Sinclair Terrace
Wick
KW1 5AB
Phone: 01955 606432
Fax: 01955 603000
www.northhighlandarchive.org

North Lanarkshire Archive
10 Kelvin Road
Lenziemill
Cumbernauld
G67 2BA
Phone: 01236 737 114
Fax: 01236 781 762
www.northlan.gov.uk

Orkney Archives
The Orkney Library
Laing Street
Kirkwall
KW15 1NW
Phone: 01856 873166
Fax: 01856 875260

Perth and Kinross District Archive
AK Bell Library
2-8 York Place
Perth
PH2 8EP
Phone: 01738 477012
Fax: 01738 477010
www.pkc.gov.uk/library/archive.htm

Scottish Borders Archive and Local
  History Centre
St Mary's Mill
Selkirk
TD7 5EU
Phone: 01750 724903
Fax: 01750 22875

Shetland Archives
44 King Harald Street
Lerwick
ZE1 0EQ
Phone: 01595 696247
Fax: 01595 696533
www.shetland.gov.uk/

South Lanarkshire Archives
Records Management Unit
30 Hawbank Road
College Milton
East Kilbride
G74 5EX
Phone: 01355 239193
Fax: 01355 242365
www.southlanarkshire.gov.uk

Stirling Council Archives Services
Unit 6
Burghmuir Industrial Estate
Stirling
FK7 7PY
Phone: 01786 450745
Fax: 01786 443005
www.stirling.gov.uk

West Lothian Council Archives
7 Rutherford Square
Brucefield Industrial Estate
Bellsquarry
Livingston
West Lothian
EH54 9BU
Phone: 01506 460 020
Fax: 01506 416 167
www.westlothian.gov.uk/libraries

University Archives

University of Aberdeen
Special Libraries and Archives
King's College
Aberdeen
AB24 3SW
Phone: 01224 272598
Fax: 01224 273891
www.abdn.ac.uk/diss/heritage

Dundee University Archives
Tower Building
University of Dundee
Dundee
DD1 4HN
Phone: 01382 344 095
Fax: 01382 345 523
www.dundee.ac.uk/archives

Edinburgh University Library: Special
  Collections Division
George Square
Edinburgh
EH8 9LJ
Phone: 0131 650 8379
Fax: 0131 650 6863
*www.lib.ed.ac.uk/lib/resources/collections/
  specdivision/*

Glasgow Caledonian University Library
  and Information Centre
Cowcaddens Road
Glasgow
G4 0BA
Phone: 0141 331 3920
Fax: 0141 331 3005
www.lib.gcal.ac.uk/speccoll/index.htm

Glasgow University Archive Services
13 Thurso Street
Glasgow
G11 6PE
Phone: 0141 330 5516
Fax: 0141 330 4158
www.archives.gla.ac.uk

Heriot-Watt University Archives
Riccarton
Currie
Edinburgh
EH14 4AS
Phone: 0131 449 3219
Fax: 0131 451 3164
www.hw.ac.uk/archive

St Andrews University Library
Department of Manuscripts
North Street
St Andrews
KY16 9TR
Phone: 01334 462324
Fax: 01334 462282
http://specialcollections.st-and.ac.uk

Stirling University Library and Special
  Collections
Stirling
FK9 4LA
Phone: 01786 467 236
Fax: 01786 466 866
www.library.stir.ac.uk/spcoll/index.html

Strathclyde University Archives
University of Strathclyde
McCance Building
16 Richmond Street
Glasgow
G1 1XQ
Phone: 0141 548 2397
Fax: 0141 552 0775
www.strath.ac.uk/Departments/Archives/

Medical Archives

Dumfries and Galloway Health Board
  Archives
Easterbrook Hall
Crichton Royal Hospital
Dumfries
DG1 4TG
Phone: 01387 244 228
Fax: 01387 269 696

NHS Greater Glasgow Archive
77-87 Dumbarton Road
Glasgow
G11 6PW
Phone: 0141 330 2992
Fax: 0141 330 4158
www.archives.gla.ac.uk/gghb/

Lothian Health Services Archive
Special Collections
Edinburgh University Library
George Square
Edinburgh
EH8 9LJ
Phone: 0131 650 3392
Fax: 0131 650 6863
www.lhsa.lib.ed.ac.uk/

Northern Health Services Archives
Aberdeen Royal Infirmary
Woolmanhill
Aberdeen
AB25 1LD
Phone: 01224 555562

Royal College of Nursing Archives
Scottish Board
42 South Oswald Road
Edinburgh
EH9 2HH
Phone: 0131 662 1010
Fax: 0131 662 1032
www.qmuc.ac.uk/hn/history/index.htm

Royal College of Physicians and Surgeons of Glasgow
234-242 St Vincent Street
Glasgow
G2 5RJ
Phone: 0141 227 3234
www.rcpsglasg.ac.uk/archives.html

Royal College of Physicians of Edinburgh
9 Queen Street
Edinburgh
EH2 1JQ
Phone: 0131 225 7324
Fax: 0131 220 3939
www.rcpe.ac.uk

Royal College of Surgeons of Edinburgh
Nicolson Street
Edinburgh
EH8 9DW
Phone: 0131 527 1630
Fax: 0131 557 6406
www.rcsed.ac.uk

Genealogical Societies

Aberdeen and North East Scotland
  Family History Society
164 King Street
Aberdeen
AB24 5BD
Phone: 01224 646323
Fax: 01224 639096
www.anesfhs.org.uk

Alloway & Southern Ayrshire Family
  History Society
c/o Alloway Library
Doonholm Road
Ayr
KA7 4QQ
www.maybole.org/history/resources/
  asafhs.htm

Association of Scottish Genealogists and
  Record Agents (ASGRA)
93 Colinton Road
Edinburgh
EH4 1ET
www.asgra.co.uk

Borders Family History Society
2 Fellowhills
Ladykirk
Berwickshire
TD15 1XN
www.vivdunstan.clara.net/genuki/misc/
  bordersFHS.html

Caithness Family History Society
Mill Cottage
Corsback
Dunnet
Caithness
KW14 8XQ
www.caithnessfhs.org.uk

Central Scotland Family History Society
11 Springbank Gardens
Dunblane
FK15 9JX
www.csfhs.org.uk

Dumfries and Galloway Family History
  Society
Family History Centre
9 Glasgow Street
Dumfries
DG2 9AF
www.dgfhs.org.uk

East Ayrshire Family History Society
c/o The Dick Institute
Elmbank Ave
Kilmarnock
KA1 3BU
www.eastayrshirefhs.org.uk

Fife Family History Society
Glenmoriston
Durie Street
Leven
Fife
KY8 4HF
www.fifefhs.org

The Genealogy Society of Utah
Family History Support Office
185 Penns Lane
Sutton Coalfield
West Midlands
B75 1JU
www.familysearch.org

Glasgow & West of Scotland Family
   History Society
Unit 5, 22 Mansfield Street
Glasgow
G11 5QP
www.gwsfhs.org.uk

Guild of One-Name Studies
The Hon Secretary
Box G, 14 Charterhouse Buildings
Goswell Road
London
EC1M 7BA
www.one-name.org

The Heraldry Society of Scotland
2/6 Huntingdon Place
Edinburgh
EH7 4AT
www.heraldry-scotland.co.uk

Highland Family History Society
c/o Reference Room
Public Library
Farraline Park
Inverness
IV1 INH
*www.genuki.org.uk/big/scot/
   Highland.FHS.home.html*

Lanarkshire Family History Society
c/o Local History Room
Motherwell Heritage Centre
High Road
Motherwell
North Lanarkshire
ML1 3HU
www.lanarkshirefhs.org.uk

Largs and North Ayrshire Family History
   Society
12 Kelvin Gardens
Largs
Ayrshire
KA30 3SX
*www.freeyellow.com/members7/lnafhs/
   index.html*

The Lothian Family History Society
c/o Lasswade High School Centre
Eskdale Drive
Bonnyrigg
Midlothian
EH19 2LA
www.lothiansfhs.org.uk

Orkney Family History Society
Strynd Community Room
Kirkwall
KW15 1HG
www.genuki.org.uk/big/sct/OKI/ofhs.html

Renfrewshire Family History Society
c/o Paisley Museum & Art Galleries
High Street
Paisley
PA1 2BA
Tel: 0141 889 3151
www.renfrewshirefhs.org.uk

Scottish Association of Family History
   Societies
51/3 Mortonhall Road
Edinburgh
EH9 2HN
www.safhs.org.uk

The Scottish Genealogy Society
15 Victoria Terrace
Edinburgh
EH1 2JL
Phone/Fax: 0131 220 3677
www.scotsgenealogy.com

Shetland Family History Society
6 Hillhead
Lerwick
Shetland
ZE1 0EJ
www.shetland-fhs.org.uk

Tay Valley Family History Society
Research Centre
179–181 Princes Street
Dundee
DD4 6DQ
Phone: 01382 461845
www.tayvalleyfhs.org.uk

Troon @ Ayrshire Family History Society
c/o M.E.R.C. Troon Public Library
South Beach
Troon
Ayrshire
KA10 6EF
www.troonayrshirefhs.org.uk

West Lothian Family History Society
23 Templar Rise
Livingstone
EH54 6PJ
www.wlfhs.org.uk

ᐧᐧ *Appendix B* ᐧᐧ
Useful Books

Various published works are recommended at appropriate points in the text. The following list repeats some of the more useful of them and also suggests further publications which you may wish to consult. The names of publishers are placed in brackets.

Annual Report of the Keeper of the Records of Scotland (Copies may be purchased from the National Archives of Scotland, or viewed on *www.nas.gov.uk.*)

British Genealogical Microfiche by Stuart A Raymond (Federation of Family History Societies)

The Concise Scots Dictionary (Scottish National Dictionary Association/Polygon at Edinburgh)

The Genealogist's Internet by Peter Christian (The National Archives)

Genealogy for Beginners by Arthur Willis (Phillimore & Co)

Guide to the National Archives of Scotland (The Stationery Office/Stair Society)

In Search of Scottish Ancestry by Gerald Hamilton-Edwards (Phillimore)

Index of Scottish Place Names from 1981 Census (The Stationery Office)

My Ain Folk by Graham S Holton and Jack Winch (Tuckwell Press)

National Index of Parish Registers, Volume XII: Sources for Scottish Genealogy and Family History by D J Steel (Phillimore, for Society of Genealogists)

Netting Your Ancestors by Cyndi Howells (Genealogical Publishing Company Inc)

The New Statistical Account of Scotland (15 volumes, published 1845. Electronic version available at *http://edina.ac.uk/statacc/*)

An Ordinary of Arms contained in the Public Register of all Arms and Bearings in Scotland by Sir James Balfour Paul (Genealogical Publishing Company, Inc)

The Parishes, Registers and Registrars of Scotland by S M Spiers (ed) (Scottish Association of Family History Societies)

Scotland. A Genealogical Research Guide (LDS, Family History Library)

Scottish Ancestry Research: A Brief Guide by Donald Whyte (Scotpress)

Scottish Family Histories by Joan P S Ferguson (National Library of Scotland)

Scottish Family History by Margaret Stuart and Sir James Balfour Paul (Oliver & Boyd; reprinted by Genealogical Publishing Company, Baltimore)

Scottish Family History by David Moody (Genealogical Publishing Company, Inc)

The Scottish Genealogist, the quarterly journal of the Scottish Genealogy Society (address in Appendix A)

The Statistical Account of Scotland compiled by Sir John Sinclair (21 volumes, published 1791-1799. Electronic version available at *http://edina.ac.uk/statacc/*)

The Surnames of Scotland by George F Black (The New York Public Library)

Tracing Scottish Ancestors by Rosemary Bigwood (HarperCollins)

Tracing Your Ancestors in the Public Record Office by Jane Cox and Timothy Padfield (The Stationery Office)

Tracing Your Ancestors in Northern Ireland by Ian Maxwell, edited by Grace McGrath (The Stationery Office)

Tracing Your Scottish Ancestry by Kathleen B Cory (Polygon)

Using Death and Burial Records for Family Historians by Lilian Gibbens (Federation of Family History Societies)

Wills and Where to Find Them by T W S Gibson (Phillimore)

Your Scottish Ancestry: A Guide for North Americans by Sherry Irvine (Ancestry Incorporated)

A list of NAS publications will be sent on request, or may be viewed on the NAS website bookshop at *www.nas.gov.uk*.

Many useful calendars and indices of Scottish records have been and are being published by the Scottish Record Society. For a list of available titles, see *www.scottishrecordsociety.org* or contact the Honorary Secretary, Professor James Kirk, Department of Scottish History, University of Glasgow, Glasgow G12 8QQ. The Society's earlier publications are unfortunately out of print.

❦ *Index* ❧
to Classes and Types
of Records

Index
to Categories of
Individuals

A

Accidents, persons involved in, 7.31; 13.45; 24.50
Accountant of the Court, 27.8
Accused persons, 14.4–5, 9, 23
Adopted children, 7.15
Advocate Deputes, 16.2
Advocates, 13.10; 16.2; 21.1-2
Airmen, 17.21–22
America, emigrants to, 13.20; 28.16, 18
Apprentices, 17.6; 21.5; 25.1-7
Architects, 22.1-3
Artists, 22.1
Asylums, inmates in, 27.3, 9-13
Australia, emigrants to, 29.3, 5; prisoners transported to, 14.25

B

Bachelors, 15.8
Bankrupts, 13.26–29, 58-59
Bastards, *see* illegitimate children
Baxters, 25.3
Burgesses, 25.1-2
Burgh councillors, 26.1, 4

C

Canada, emigrants to, 29.3, 6
Carters, 25.3
Catholics *see* Roman Catholics
Chemists, 20.4
Church of Scotland members, 4.27; 18.1; ministers, clergymen, 15.6; 18.1, 3, 8

Coal miners, 24.1-5
Commissary clerks, 16.1
Congregational Church, members of, 7.2
Convicts, 14.25
Cordiners, 25.4
Cottars, 11.14; 29.6
County councillors, 26.4
Courts, staff of, 16.2, 3
Craftsmen, 25.1-7
Creditors, *see* litigants
Criminals, 3.8; 13.33, 65; 14.1–29; 17.20; 27.14; 29.2
Crofters, 11.1-15; 29.6
Curators, 9.21; 27.4-8
Customs officers, 16.4-6

D

Debtors, *see* litigants, prisoners
Dentists, 18.4
Destitute, 28.4, 25
Disabled, 28.3, 11
Divinity students, 18.2
Doctors, 20.1-2
Dyers, 25.3-4

E

Edinburgh Castle, governors of, 16.2
Elders of the Kirk, 18.7
Electors, 10.51; 26.1-7
Emigrants, 29.1-6
Episcopalians, 7.1-2; 18.10
Exchequer, Court of, staff of, 16.2-3
Excise officers, *see* customs officers
Executors, 8.3, 7, 10, 13-14, 25-26

210

Tutors, 9.5, 7, 10, 13, 20-21; 13.25;
    27.4, 10

U

Unitarians, 7.2
United Free Church, members of, 7.2;
    ministers of, 18.1
United Presbyterian Church, ministers
    of, 18.1
University students and staff, 19.6-7

V

Vassals, 9.23; 13.51
Victims of crime, 14.20–14.21
Voters, *see* electors

W

Whale fishing, seamen engaged in, 17.17
Weavers, 25.3, 5
Witnesses, 4.21; 10.11, 32; 14.3–5, 11,
    18, 20; 18.7
Wrights, 25.3
Writers (lawyers), 21.1-3